Good Jobs, Bad Jobs

Canadian Cataloguing in Publication Data

Main entry under title:

Good jobs, bad jobs: employment in the service economy;
a statement

Issued also in French under title: L'emploi au futur.
ISBN 0-660-13458-6
DSS cat. no. EC22-164/1990E

1. Labor supply – Canada. 2. Service industries –
Canada. 3. Canada – Industries. 4. Employment
forecasting – Canada. I. Economic Council of
Canada. II. Title: Employment in the service economy.

HD5728.G66 1990   331.12'0971   C90-098539-9

Good Jobs, Bad Jobs

Employment in the Service Economy

A Statement by the
Economic Council of Canada
1990

© Minister of Supply and Services Canada 1990

Available in Canada through

Associated Bookstores
and other booksellers

or by mail from

Canadian Government Publishing Centre
Supply and Services Canada
Ottawa, Canada K1A 0S9

Catalogue No. EC22-164/1990E
ISBN 0-660-13458-6

Contents

Members of the Economic Council of Canada	vii
Foreword	ix
Introduction	1
The Service Economy	2
Classifying the Service Industries	2
Dynamic Services	2
Traditional Services	2
Nonmarket Services	2
Technology and the Changing Nature of Services	2
The Convergence between Goods and Services	4
Services and the Job-Creation Process	4
The Growth of Service Employment	4
The Linkages between Goods and Services	5
Simulation Results	5
Input/Output Analysis	6
Nonmarket Services	8
The Internationalization of Services	8
Trade in Services	9
Employment Impact	9
Conclusion	10
The New Job Market	10
Nature of the Emerging Job Structure	10
Location of Jobs	10
Nonstandard Employment	11
Skill Trends	13
Earnings Trends	14
Adjusting to the Changing Job Structure	16
Older Workers	16
Poorly Educated Workers	17
Laid-Off Workers	17
Conclusion	17
Conclusions and Policy Implications	18
Strengthen the Commitment to the Development of Human Resources	19
Education	19
Training and Labour Adjustment	20
Policies Aimed at "Unattached" Workers	21
Employer-Based Human-Resource Development	24

Promote Economic Security for Workers		26
Employment Standards		27
Public Benefit Programs		27
Pensions		27
Recognize the Role of Services in Economic Growth		28
Industrial Policy		28
Linking Goods and Services		28
Service Infrastructure		29
Regional Development		30
Measuring the Service Economy		30

Comments   33

Project Staff   35

Tables

1	Employment Shares and Employment Growth, by Industry, 1967-88	5
2	Exports and Export-Dependent Employment in Dynamic Services, 1988	9
3	Index of Employment Concentration in Selected Cities and Towns, Dynamic Services, 1986	11
4	Information-Based Employment, 1971-86	14
5	Median Earnings of the Labour Force and Distribution by Earnings Level, 1967-86	14
6	Middle-Income Families, 1967-86	15
7	Long-Term Unemployment, by Age Group, 1981 and 1987	16
8	Public Expenditure on Labour Market Programs, Selected Countries, 1987	21

Charts

1	Contribution of Major Sectors to Employment Growth, 1967-88	5
2	Proportion of Output Sold as Intermediate Input, by Service Industry, 1985	6
3	Impact of the Goods-Producing Industries on the Service Sector, 1985	7
4	Impact of the Service Industries on the Goods-Producing Sector, 1985	8
5	Growth in the Relative Importance of Part-Time Employment, by Province, 1975-88	12
6	Labour Force Growth, 1960-2000	13
7	Proportion of Workers in Nonstandard Employment, by Major Sector, 1986	13
8	Distribution of Job Separators by the Number of Weeks of Joblessness, 1986	16
9	Level of Schooling and Rate of Unemployment, 1975-88	17
10	Job Changes and Wage Loss, 1986	17

This Statement reflects the views of the Members of the Economic Council of Canada; however, comments from Peter Brophey, Chester Johnson, and Graham Wilson, appear at the end of the document.

Members of the Economic Council of Canada

JUDITH MAXWELL, Chairman
CAROLINE PESTIEAU, Deputy Chairman and Director
HARVEY LAZAR, Deputy Chairman and Director

MILLER H. AYRE
   President and Chief Executive Officer
   Ayre's Limited
   St. John's

DIANE BELLEMARE
   Professor, Economics Department
   Université du Québec à Montréal
   Montréal

JALYNN H. BENNETT
   President
   Jalynn H. Bennett Associates Ltd.
   Toronto

ALAN A. BORGER
   President
   Ladco Company Limited
   Winnipeg

JACQUES BOUGIE
   President and Chief Operating Officer
   Alcan Aluminium Limited
   Montréal

PETER M. BROPHEY
   Vice-President, Corporate Affairs
   Xerox Canada Inc.
   North York

DIAN COHEN
   President
   Dian Cohen Productions
   Aurora

THOMAS J. COURCHENE
   Director
   School of Policy Studies
   Queen's University
   Kingston

LÉON COURVILLE
   Executive Vice-President
   National Bank of Canada
   Montréal

ALIX GRANGER
   Vice President
   Pemberton, Houston, Willoughby, Inc.
   Vancouver

YVES GUÉRARD
   President
   Groupe Sobeco Inc.
   Montréal

CHESTER A. JOHNSON
   Chairman and Chief Executive Officer
   Western Pulp Inc.
   Vancouver

WILLIAM MACKNESS
   Dean, Faculty of Management
   University of Manitoba
   Winnipeg

MARCEL PEPIN
   Professor
   École de Relations industrielles
   Université de Montréal
   Montréal

STRUAN ROBERTSON
   Chairman
   Central Guaranty Trust Company
   Halifax

BARTLETT B. ROMBOUGH
   President and Chief Executive Officer
   PanCanadian Petroleum Limited
   Calgary

KEN W. STICKLAND
   President
   KenAgra Management Services Ltd.
   Edmonton

MICHAEL A. SULLIVAN
   Chartered Accountant
   Summerside

NORMAN E. WALE
   Vice-President
   Investor and Industry Relations
   Canadian Pacific Limited
   Montréal

H. GRAHAM WILSON
   Vice-President and Secretary
   Dofasco Inc.
   Hamilton

Foreword

The Council launched its study of employment in the service economy in late 1987 because it was clear that Canadians needed to know more about the sector that has been generating virtually all of the new jobs in Canada.

The results go well beyond our expectations. For we have sketched out a portrait here of a "new" labour market, one where jobs are created in different ways, where different skills are required, and where work is being compensated differently. What is more, we found that many of these changes are also occurring in resources and manufacturing. This leads us to suspect that work in general is being transformed by systemic changes such as new technologies and new ways of organizing production. It will take further research to spell out all of the underlying forces, but we can say with some conviction, at this stage, that we have identified some profound changes in the content of work and in how it is organized.

Such a fundamental shift in labour markets obviously has major economic and social repercussions that go to the heart of individual well-being, social mobility, and income distribution. We find, therefore, that our recommendations touch a number of areas of public policy. In some cases, such as education, pensions, and industrial and regional policy, we can make only general observations and set out warning signals. More monitoring and research will be needed in the next few years.

In other areas, such as training and employment standards, we have enough evidence to recommend substantive changes in policy, and, in some cases, in the role of government. Ultimately, our analysis suggests that many of Canada's traditional institutions and patterns of behaviour must be reshaped in order to build competitive industries and to enhance the security of Canadian workers. These findings will help to shape debate on the future direction of labour market policy which has been focussed for the past six months in a series of national consultations on training and labour adjustment.

This Statement by Council members highlights the main research findings and sets out our policy advice. It will be followed by a more detailed research report and a number of in-depth background studies prepared by Council staff and experts working on contract. This new body of work builds on the research carried out under the Service Industries Studies Program by the federal Department of Industry, Science and Technology, and thus helps to extend our still rather limited knowledge of the dynamics of this diverse group of industries which have come to play such an important role in the Canadian economy.

The project was ably conceived and directed by Gordon Betcherman, the Project Leader, and was guided by an Advisory Committee, chaired by Diane Bellemare, which included three Council members and five outside experts. On behalf of the Council, I would like to thank the members of the Advisory Committee for volunteering their time and energy.

Their advice has helped to shape both the structure of the Statement and our interpretation of the research.

Judith Maxwell
Chairman

Good Jobs, Bad Jobs

READER'S NOTE

The reader should note that various conventional symbols similar to those used by Statistics Canada have been used in the tables:

  ..   figures not available
  ...   figures not appropriate or not applicable
  – – amount too small to be expressed
  –   nil or zero
  e   estimated figures
  x   data confidential, to meet the secrecy requirements of the *Statistics Act*.

Details may not add up to totals because of rounding.

Introduction

Canada owes its early development to the efforts of "hewers of wood" and "drawers of water." Over the past three decades, however, service activities have become the mainstay of the economy and now account for an ever-increasing share of output. The result is a profound change in the source of economic success. No longer can prosperity come straight out of the ground: increasingly, it must come from the minds of the Canadian people.

In this Statement, we focus on the effects that this transformation has had on the employment of Canadians. The expansion of service employment has been striking. In the late 1940s, 60 per cent of the Canadian labour force worked in the goods sector – natural resources, manufacturing, and construction. Today – barely one work life later – over 70 per cent of workers are employed in services. And the shift is far from over: during the 1980s, virtually all of the net job creation in this country took place in the service sector.

Given the extent of those quantitative changes, surprisingly little attention has been paid to the growth of services and to its impact on the nature of economic activity. Only within the last few years has the analysis of services in Canada begun to gather momentum; one recent example is a major service-industry study sponsored by the federal government. As more attention is being focused on this area, two basic messages emerge. First, many of the conventional concepts and measures used to understand economic events do not capture service activity very well. And second, some long-standing approaches to economic policy need refashioning.

The Council has two objectives in this Statement. The first is to summarize the results of our research on the employment changes that have occurred as the industrial structure of the Canadian economy has been transformed. That research focused on three questions:

- What factors determine job creation in a service economy?

- What are the distributional impacts of the emerging job structure?

- What role does human-resource development play in a service economy?

In its studies, the Council has used a variety of analytical approaches, drawn both from economics and from other social sciences; we have relied on a number of different information sources, ranging from census data and other Statistics Canada databases to special surveys and case studies sponsored by the Council itself.

Our second objective is to consider whether public policy has kept up with the changing labour market. We conclude that it has not and that many of Canada's traditional institutions and policy approaches in this area do indeed require some refitting. To offer a direction for the future, we identify three general and mutually reinforcing principles that must be at the centre of any strategy to achieve high employment and maximize the contribution of human resources in an economy where services play such a central role:

1 *Strengthen the commitment to the development of human resources.* In the emerging economy, universal attainment of basic skills, the development of excellence through highly qualified personnel, and widespread access to retraining opportunities are becoming imperative. To meet the challenges of the global marketplace and the economic expectations of its people, Canada simply must be a world leader with respect to the quality of its work force. This will require fundamental changes in the country's commitment and approach to education and training.

2 *Promote economic security for workers.* A number of forces are acting to increase the "segmentation" of the labour market, with employment experiences becoming increasingly polarized into two categories – "good" jobs and "bad" jobs. One source of segmentation has been the growth of "nonstandard" work. As both part-time and short-term jobs become more common, labour policies must better reflect this new diversity if they are to provide security for growing numbers of Canadians in nonstandard employment.

3 *Recognize the role of services in economic growth.* The service sector is now a vital component of the Canadian economy in terms of both its domestic and international dimensions. At the same time, the growth in the size of the service sector does not mean that Canada is "de-industrializing": goods production remains an important component of overall output. Indeed, both goods and services make critical and increasingly interdependent contributions to economic prosperity. Successful development strategies – both national and regional – will have to maintain strong resource and manufacturing industries and foster a high-quality and innovative service sector.

* * * * *

In this Statement, we first describe the service sector and the industries that it includes. We then explore the process of job creation in a service economy, and go on to focus on the nature of the emerging job structure. And finally, we turn to the policy implications of our analysis and to the three principles highlighted above.

The Service Economy

Economists have traditionally distinguished between "goods" and "services." The goods-producing sector consists of *primary* industries – which include agriculture, fishing, forestry, and mining (including oil and gas) – and *secondary* industries, which include manufacturing and construction. The service, or *tertiary*, sector represents the remainder of the economy. Services have traditionally been characterized as intangible, nontransferable, and nonstorable; as well, the conventional view of services involves direct contact between the producer and the consumer. Innovations in technology and industrial organization, however, are changing the nature of both goods and services to the point where the borderline between the two activities is becoming blurred.

Classifying the Service Industries

The service sector includes a wide range of diverse industries; accordingly, we have organized it into three subsectors (see box). Each of these subsectors has its own distinctive characteristics and employment patterns.

Dynamic Services

The dynamic subsector includes four major industry divisions: two of these are distribution-oriented (transportation, communications, and utilities; and wholesale trade), and two are commercially oriented (finance, insurance, and real estate; and business services). These industries share a number of characteristics that contribute to their dynamic nature. They are high-value-added industries that, for the most part, have become more and more involved in internationally competitive markets. Not only is trade in dynamic services growing in importance, but these services are becoming critical ingredients in the production and distribution of goods.

Traditional Services

The traditional subsector consists of retail trade, accommodation and food, and personal services (which include a grab-bag of activities from haircutting, cleaning, and repairing to amusement and recreation). These industries are "traditional" in the sense that they represent the old "Main Street" variety of services. It would be a mistake, however, not to recognize the changes that are taking place within this subsector. Most notable, perhaps, has been the emergence of megacorporations – in the fast-food industry, for example – and their progressive application of mass, standardized production technologies, inventory systems, and marketing techniques. In retailing, to offer another example, we observe commercial innovations, such as self-service and at-home buying.

Nevertheless, the traditional services remain, on balance, largely insulated from the trends towards globalization and international competitiveness that are driving the goods sector and the dynamic-service subsector. Much of the traditional-service subsector still tends to operate in local or, at most, national markets; compared with dynamic services, value-added is lower in traditional services; there is less emphasis on productivity growth; and the role of technological change is less pronounced.

Nonmarket Services

The third subsector – nonmarket services – includes education, health, social services, and public administration. While competition has traditionally not been a significant factor in this subsector, nonmarket services are relevant to economic competitiveness, for two reasons. First, the efficiency with which these services are produced will affect the level of public financing that is needed. And second, nonmarket services provide inputs into the activity of all private-sector firms. Those inputs include, for example, infrastructure (such as transportation and communication systems), education and health (which have an important bearing on the quality of the work force), and regulatory services. As a result, the nature of nonmarket services itself has been changing, with more attention now being paid to such matters as productivity growth and technological change.

Technology and the Changing Nature of Services

As noted earlier, traditional views of the service sector need to be reappraised in light of the rapid technological and organizational innovations that are transforming the economy. Of particular relevance in this respect has been the development, application, and diffusion of "telematics" – interrelated computer and telecommunications technologies. These technologies are transforming both the nature of service activities and the contribution that they make to economic growth.

The Structure of the Service Sector*

Dynamic Services

Transportation, communications, and utilities
   Air, rail, and water transport
   Ground transportation
   Pipelines
   Storage and warehousing
   Broadcasting – radio, television, cable
   Telephone systems
   Postal and courier services
   Utilities – electricity, gas, water, and sewage systems
Wholesale trade
Finance, insurance, and real estate
   Banks and trust companies
   Credit unions and mortgage companies
   Insurance companies
   Investment dealers
   Real estate operators
Business services
   Employment agencies
   Advertising services
   Architectural, scientific, engineering, and computing services
   Legal services
   Management consulting

Traditional Services

Retail trade
   Food stores
   Drug stores and liquor stores
   Shoe and clothing stores
   Furniture, appliance, furnishings, and stereo stores
   Car dealers, gas stations, and auto repair shops
   Department stores
   Jewellery stores and photographic stores
Personal services
   Hotels
   Restaurants and bars
   Film, audio, and video production and distribution
   Movie houses and theatres
   Barber and beauty shops
   Laundries and cleaners
   Funeral services
   Machinery and car rental companies
   Photographers
   Repair shops (excluding auto)
   Building security services
   Travel agencies

Nonmarket Services

Education services
   Schools, colleges, and universities
   Libraries, museums, and archives
Health services
   Hospitals
   Nursing homes
   Doctors and dentists
   Medical laboratories
Social services
   Daycare, meal services, and crisis centres
   Psychologists and social workers
   Religious organizations
Public administration

*For data-related reasons, this classification scheme has been organized within the framework of Statistics Canada's Standard Industrial Classification.

Indeed, because of technological changes, some of the conventionally held views on the distinctive features of service activity are becoming less relevant. For example, information-based services are increasingly transferable through digital telecommunications systems, and some services – software programs and expert systems, for example – are now storable. As a consequence, direct contact between the producer and consumer is no longer necessary for more and more service transactions.

Technological change, particularly in telematics, has also generated new types of information-based service activities. Computers have created the potential for the collection and analysis of huge amounts of complex information quickly and cheaply. At the same time, revolutionary progress in telecommunications has made it possible to link physically separated units through information-transmission systems. The ability to process and communicate vast amounts of information quickly has become recognized as a valuable tool; that recognition, in turn, has generated a demand for even greater quantities of information.

The nature and scale of service activity in the late 20th century are entangled, then, in the growth of information demand, information-processing technologies, suppliers of information-based products, and the physical infrastructure that allows the transmission of information. Canada, along with the other developed countries, is witnessing a major transformation of its economic structure, reflected in the growth of service activities throughout the economy and mediated through computer and telecommunications technologies.

The Convergence between Goods and Services

The convergence between goods and services, alluded to above, reflects three developments. First, as noted above, technological changes are blurring the conventional distinctive features of a growing number of service activities. Second, goods production is becoming more "service-like." Increasingly, job growth in the goods sector is in white-collar occupations, which provide services such as administration, information collection and processing, research and development, marketing, and clerical work. As well, some recent innovations – e.g., just-in-time and customized production methods – endow goods production with service-like features, such as nonstorability and direct contact between the producer and the consumer. And third, the growing trend towards "bundling" services and goods together in an integrated package – incorporating training and maintenance contracts into equipment sales is one example – is also acting as a converging force.

* * * * *

While these trends are blurring the distinction between goods and services, some of the employment trends discussed in this Statement – in terms of job-creation patterns, job location, and employment forms, for example – are related, at least in part, to the shift to services. For this reason, the following analysis focuses particularly on developments in the service sector. We have found, however, that a number of forces – including technological innovation and the information revolution, globalization, and the changing composition of the work force – are fundamentally affecting employment in all industries. Accordingly, when we turn to policy issues at the end of this Statement, our discussion will be broadened to consider, in its entirety, the new labour market that is emerging.

Services and the Job-Creation Process

What of the job-creation process in a service-dominated labour market? In examining this theme, we have been led to recognize the importance of the linkages between the goods sector and the service sector in generating economic activity and employment. Job creation in the 1990s will be dictated by the synergies between goods and services (including nonmarket services) and by the competitiveness of the country's service industries, especially in the dynamic subsector.

The Growth of Service Employment

The shift of employment from goods-producing activities to services began early in this century. Until the 1950s, however, the transition was gradual: the service sector's share of total employment rose from about 34 per cent in 1911 to 44 per cent in 1951. Since then, the pace has accelerated notably. Between 1967 and 1988, service employment increased at an average annual rate of 3.2 per cent, compared with 0.9 per cent in goods (Table 1). By 1988, 71 per cent of Canadian workers were employed in the service sector; according to our projections, that proportion will rise to 73 per cent by 1993.

The shift to services is not unique to Canada. Indeed, it has occurred in all of the major OECD countries in the postwar period, although the pace and nature of the transformation has differed from country to country.

As Chart 1 indicates, nearly 90 per cent of the job growth in Canada since 1967 has taken place in the service sector, with all of the service subsectors having made important contributions; indeed, most of them have expanded at an annual rate of about 3 per cent. By a considerable margin, the business-services industry has experienced the fastest growth; rapid gains have also been recorded in social services, health, and the finance, insurance, and real estate group.

Why has the service-sector share of employment grown so rapidly? That question is difficult to answer. A number of explanations have been put forward – that the growing share of service employment simply reflects the poorer productivity performance of the service sector relative to the goods-producing sector, for example, or that the share of final demand allocated to services has increased as incomes have risen and as more women have entered the work force. It has also been argued that the measured growth of services reflects a trend towards "contracting-out" – i.e., that the level of service activity in the economy has changed very little but that goods producers are simply now purchasing some services from outside the firm that they used to produce "in-house."

Our research indicates, however, that these factors account for only a small part of the shift to services. Instead,

Table 1

Employment Shares and Employment Growth, by Industry, 1967-88

	Industry employment		
	As a share of total employment		Annual growth rate, 1967-88
	1967	1988	
	(Per cent)		
Service sector	59.4	70.9	3.4
Dynamic services	19.7	23.0	3.2
Transportation, communications, and utilities	9.0	7.4	1.5
Wholesale trade	4.5	4.6	2.7
Finance, insurance, and real estate	4.3	5.9	4.1
Business services	1.9	5.1	7.3
Traditional services	21.7	25.7	3.3
Retail trade	12.1	13.1	2.8
Personal services	9.6	12.6	3.8
Nonmarket services	18.0	22.2	3.5
Health and social services	6.2	8.9	4.3
Education	5.8	6.6	3.2
Public administration	6.0	6.7	3.0
Goods sector	40.6	29.1	0.9
Primary industries	10.3	6.0	–0.1
Manufacturing	23.9	17.2	0.9
Construction	6.5	5.9	2.1
Both sectors	100.0	100.0	2.5

SOURCE Based on data from Statistics Canada.

Chart 1

Contribution of Major Sectors to Employment Growth, 1967-88

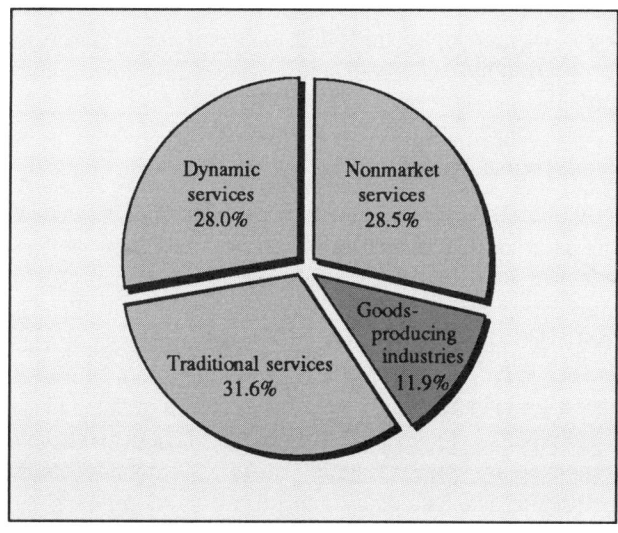

SOURCE Based on data from Statistics Canada.

our results show that the driving force has been an increase in the demand for services as inputs to production. Services have increasingly become part of the final product sold to the consumer. As Chart 2 shows, intermediate demand represents an important component of total demand, particularly for the dynamic-service industries.

The Linkages between Goods and Services

This has led us to consider the relationship between goods and services. To understand the extent to which these sectors are linked, two related exercises were undertaken. The first consisted of a series of policy simulations, using a model that was specifically designed to give an overall view of the relationship between the goods, commercial-service, and noncommercial-service sectors.

Simulation Results

One set of experiments involved changing the composition of expenditures to include a larger share of goods and

6 Good Jobs, Bad Jobs

Chart 2

Proportion of Output Sold as Intermediate Input, by Service Industry, 1985

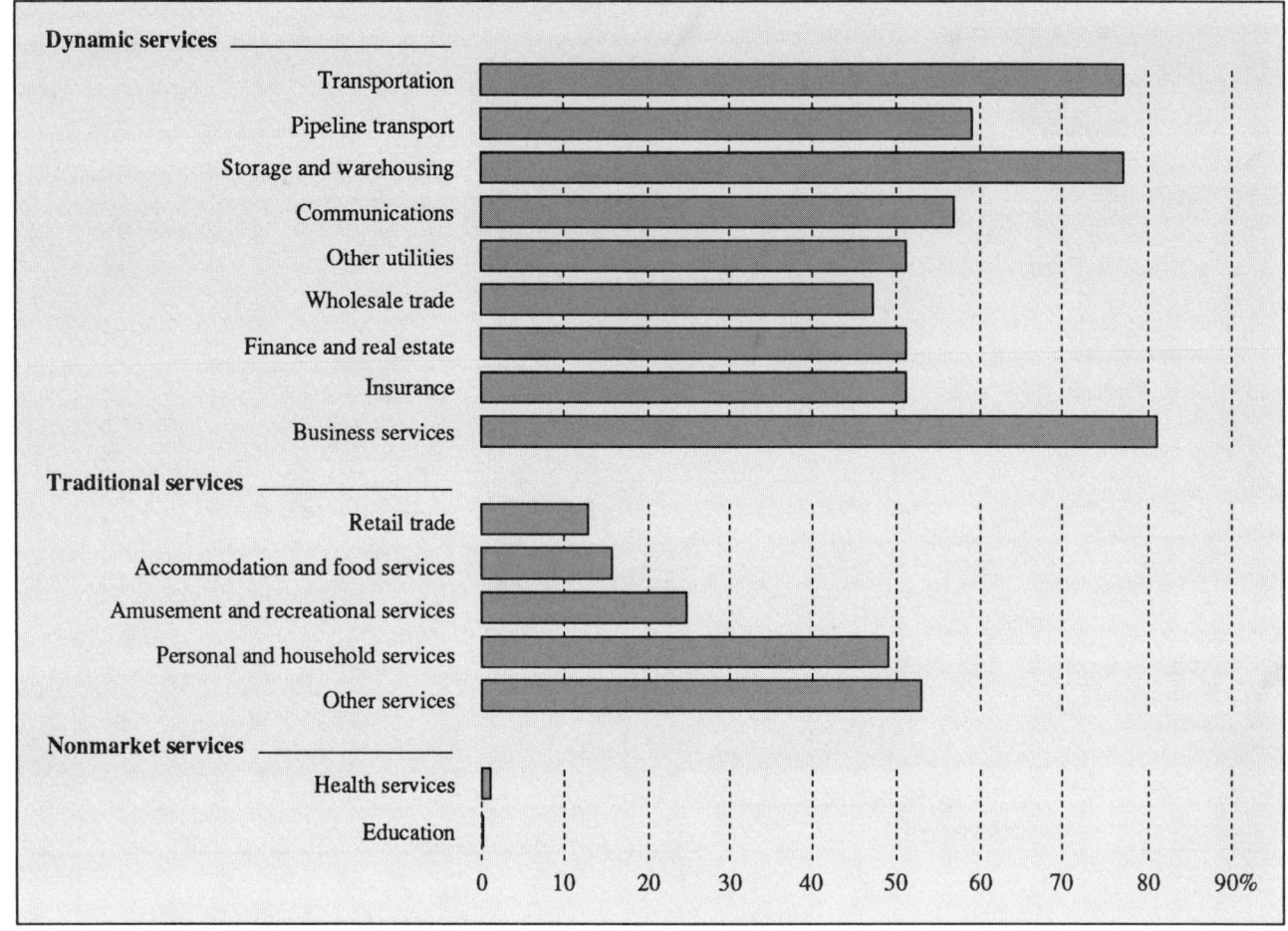

SOURCE Estimates by the Economic Council of Canada, based on data from Statistics Canada.

a correspondingly smaller share of services. Our findings were all consistent in showing that higher levels of output and employment in both the goods sector and the economy as a whole would result from such a change. In addition, the service sector would not experience any decrease in employment levels; in fact, the level of output in the commercial-service sector would increase. Clearly, the increased level of economic activity in the goods sector would stimulate growth in services as well. On the other hand, when, as part of our simulations, we stimulated services at the expense of goods, employment and output in the goods sector decreased, and the economy was weaker, on the whole.

This model is useful in providing a picture of how aggregate spending patterns affect the performance of employment and output growth. However, the fact that it contains only three broad sectors means that it cannot provide any detailed insights into *how* goods-sector growth translates into growth in the service sector. To examine that issue, we used input/output data to quantify the transactions between individual goods and commercial-service industries.

Input/Output Analysis

Our analysis showed that the stimulative influence of the goods-producing industries on services has been increasing over time: of the 28 goods industries, 25 had greater stimulative power on the service sector in 1981 than in 1971; and by 1985, most goods industries had a significant influence on output in the service sector (Chart 3). Manufacturing industries were important sources of demand for service inputs; however, even higher levels of demand were generated by some resource industries – notably, crude petroleum and natural gas, and forestry. In contrast, the stimulative power of the service industries on goods production was generally weak (Chart 4). The demand for

Chart 3

Impact of the Goods-Producing Industries on the Service Sector, 1985[1]

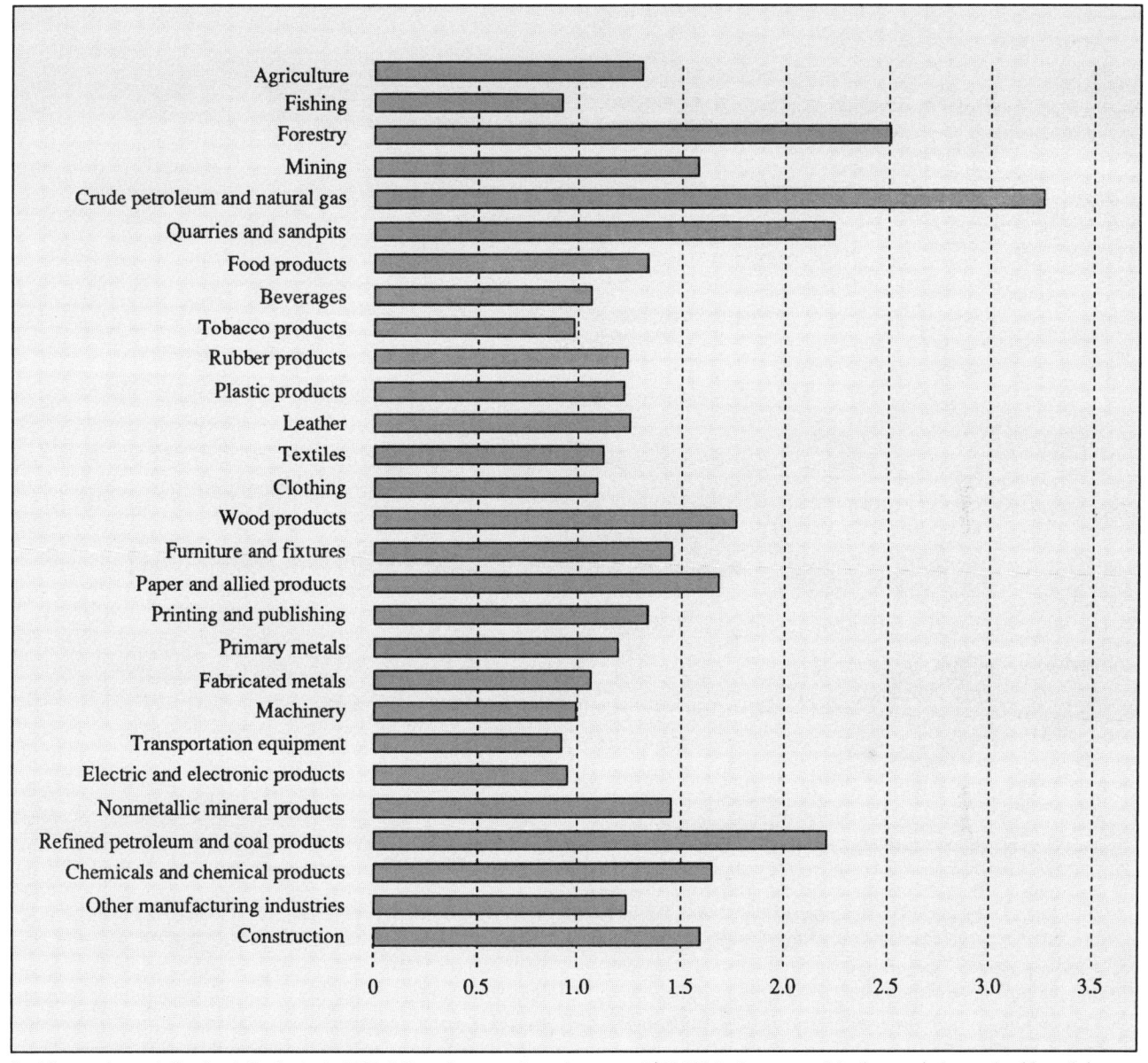

1 Measured on a dollar-for-dollar basis, in 1981 dollars; for example, an increase of $10,000 in the output of the forestry industry should result in an increase of about $2,500 in the output of the service sector.
SOURCE Estimates by the Economic Council of Canada, based on data from Statistics Canada.

goods inputs was highest in the accommodation and food-service industry, through its links to the food-production industry, and in the transportation industry.

Our analysis has emphasized the relationship between the goods industries and the dynamic services. Six service industries, which together make up the bulk of the dynamic-service subsector, were particularly dependent on demand from the goods industries for their output: finance and real estate, wholesale trade, business services, utilities, transportation, and communications. The linkages between the goods sector and the transportation, utilities, and wholesale trade industries have always been strong. One of the most striking changes in the overall structure of the economy, however, has involved the business-service, financial-service, and communications industries. These industries have shown strong employment growth and significant increases in their linkages with the goods sector.

Chart 4

Impact of the Service Industries on the Goods-Producing Sector, 1985[1]

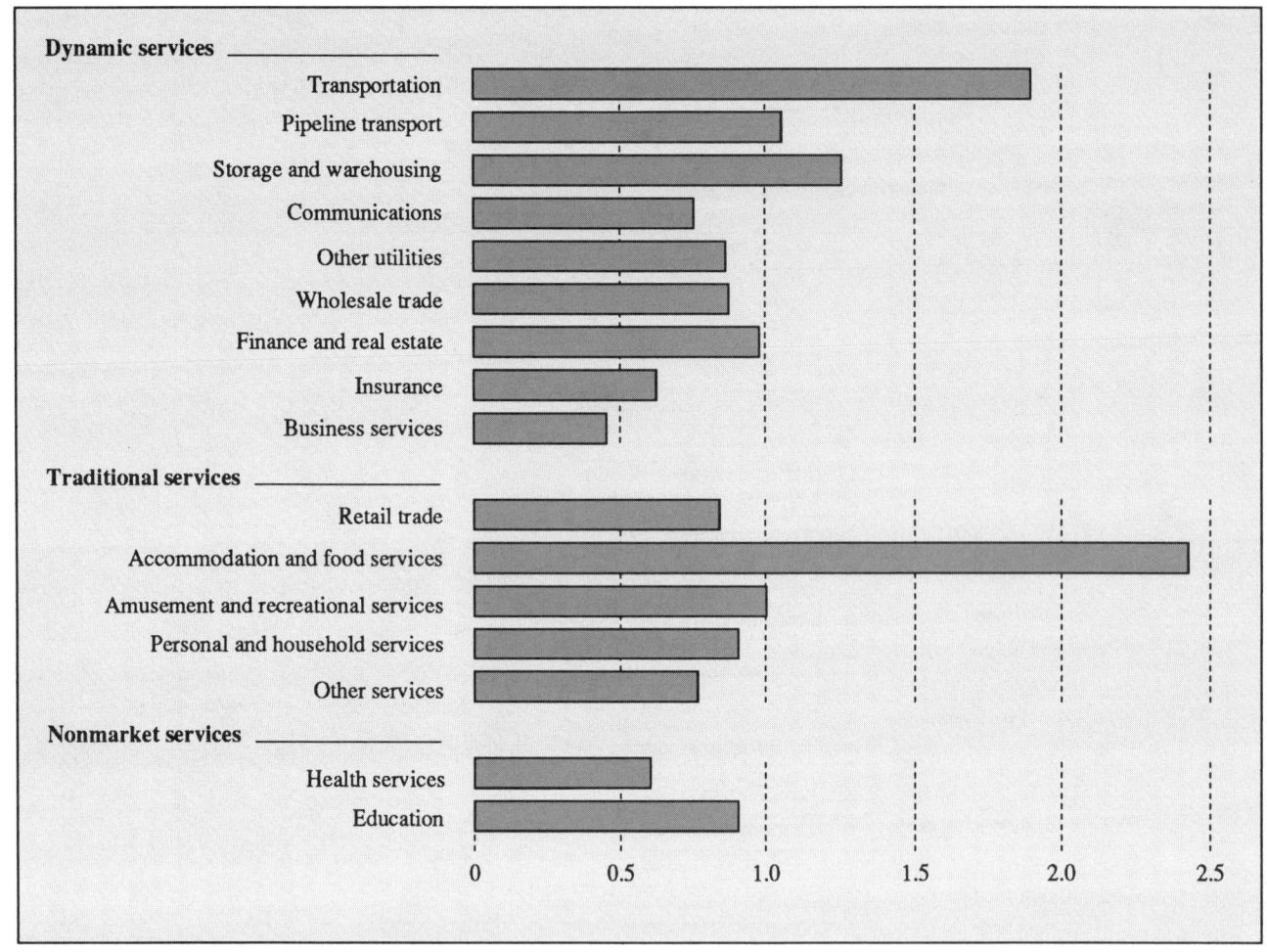

[1] Measured on a dollar-for-dollar basis, in 1981 dollars; for example, an increase of $10,000 in the output of transportation services should result in an increase of about $1,800 in the output of the goods-producing sector.
SOURCE Estimates by the Economic Council of Canada, based on data from Statistics Canada.

Technological change has played an important role in these developments by increasing the demand for information and by providing the means for satisfying that demand through those information-based services.

Clearly, the goods-producing and service sectors (especially dynamic services) are now highly interdependent: service industries need the demand originating in the goods sector, while goods industries rely heavily on the outputs of service industries as inputs to their production process.

Nonmarket Services

Government services are not included in the input/output database. As a result, the linkages between this subsector and the rest of the economy cannot be measured in the same way. However, nonmarket services also have an important influence on the production of goods. That influence is felt in many ways. For example, how governments shape the macroeconomic and regulatory environments will affect competitiveness. As well, industrial and social policies, the provision of infrastructure, education and public-sector training, and even health services are critical to the efficiency of all producers.

The Internationalization of Services

In addition to responding to the new opportunities offered by technological change in recent years, services also have been part of the global trend towards the internationalization of business activities. This is reflected, but only in part, in the data on trade in services that are discussed below. There has also been a surge, in recent years, in direct investment abroad by service industries. By 1988, foreign direct investment by Canadian service firms exceeded that of manufacturers; in contrast, only a decade earlier foreign investment by manufacturing firms was roughly four times greater. That growing presence abroad involves a wide range of services, including, for example, financial, accounting, engineering, and computer services. Canadian industry, in both the goods and service sectors, is assuming a more active multinational role, competing in an increasingly integrated global marketplace.

Trade in Services

The composition of trade in services has undergone significant changes in recent years, changes that parallel shifts in the industrial structure nationally. While the apparent effect of that trade on the level of Canadian employment is still relatively small, current trends point towards a greater impact in the future. It is the employment implications of those changes in the composition of trade, along with the growing interest in international trade in services, that are of prime interest here.

While merchandise trade can be measured quite accurately, the identification of service flows across borders is more complex, since often no physical movement takes place. Only direct exchanges of services are included in official statistics on trade in services; and even then, definitional problems arise. An important difficulty, for example, involves the distinction between service trade and investment activities. This is particularly troublesome for the banking industry, and as a consequence, trade in banking services is excluded from this discussion. The Council has, however, recently examined the Canadian financial system in the context of the internationalization of financial markets in a Statement entitled *A New Frontier* and in a companion research report entitled *Globalization and Canada's Financial Markets*.

Three points stand out when statistics on Canada's service and merchandise trade are examined. First, the volume of trade in services is small, compared with that of total merchandise trade. Second, the service trade account shows a rising deficit, and by 1987 that deficit significantly offset the surplus generated by merchandise trade. And third, the composition of service trade has been changing rapidly, and it now includes a much larger business-service component than previously, on both the export and the import side. By 1987, the business-service deficit accounted for 57 per cent of the total service deficit. Most of the trade in business services is with the United States. While Canadian exports of business services are largely in the form of arm's-length transactions and are dominated by Canadian-controlled firms, a significant proportion of imports consist of intra-corporate transactions, and half of them are by U.S.-controlled firms. At the same time, one third of business-service imports – a considerable amount – are by Canadian-controlled firms.

Employment Impact

What are the employment implications of trade in services? That question cannot be answered directly, since information on the amount of service-sector employment that is directly involved in trade is simply not available. Our approach is new and provides only a rough estimate of the magnitudes involved.

An analysis of the input/output information obtained from the 1981 Census provides the direct-export share of output for each of the dynamic-service industries (Table 2). That proportion is taken to also represent the proportion of

Table 2

Exports and Export-Dependent Employment in Dynamic Services, 1988

	Export share of total output	Export-dependent employment[1]
	(Per cent)	(Thousands)
Transportation		
Air	5.0	3
Rail	31.9	24
Truck	21.2	24
Other transportation and storage	20.3	42
Communications	2.2	5
Electric power	11.8	10
Other utilities	0.9	1
Wholesale trade	11.8	65
Finance, insurance, and real estate	1.1	7
Business services	8.7	45
All dynamic services	8.7	228

1 Estimated by multiplying the total employment in each industry by the export share of that industry's output, which is used here as a proxy for export-dependent employment.
SOURCE James McRae, "An exploratory analysis of Canada's international transactions in service commodities," a paper prepared for the Economic Council of Canada, July 1989.

employment in each of those industries that is dependent on exports. Applying those figures to the employment data for 1988, we find that nearly 230,000 jobs in the dynamic-service subsector (9 per cent of all jobs in that subsector) were directly dependent on service exports.

However, earlier studies have estimated that the magnitude of *indirect* service exports – i.e., of services "bundled" in exported goods – is about 50 per cent greater than that of direct service exports. If the effects of both direct and indirect service exports on employment are considered, then the total employment effect of service trade is more significant, as over 20 per cent of the jobs in dynamic services may then be dependent on trade. As trade in services grows and as the linkages between the goods and the service sectors continue to strengthen, the international competitiveness of Canada's service industries is likely to play an even greater role in employment in the future.

Conclusion

Two conclusions stand out from our analysis. First, sectoral interdependencies mean that a healthy goods sector is a key ingredient of total employment and output growth. By and large, goods industries operate in markets where international competition is a fact of daily life. Their competitiveness is fundamental to the demand for services. Furthermore, within the Canadian context, not only manufacturing but also the resource industries play an important role in generating demand for service inputs.

Second, services themselves are important sources of employment and output in their own right. Moreover, both commercial and nonmarket services are major contributors to overall competitiveness, since they form a large part of the inputs to goods production and since they play a key role in creating an environment that promotes competitiveness. Therefore, the quality of those services, and the quality and effectiveness of the linkages between service and goods producers, are critical for the health of the economy as a whole.

Clearly, goods and services are vital to one another. To say that the Canadian economy is either goods-based or service-based would be inaccurate; it is, in fact, an economy in which both sectors are essential to one another in a complex and linked whole. As the two become more closely linked and as each increasingly takes on features of the other, the traditional distinction between them is becoming less relevant. In many respects, goods and services are converging.

The New Job Market

The *nature* of the emerging employment structure is an issue that has become quite controversial. While the kinds of jobs that are typical in a service economy have been described in very positive terms by some and in very negative terms by others, our analysis leads us to paint a mixed portrait. Virtually all of the recent employment growth has involved either highly skilled, well-compensated, and secure jobs or unstable and relatively poorly paid jobs.

Nature of the Emerging Job Structure

Location of Jobs

Some observers believe that the growth in the size of the service sector holds out the possibility of reducing regional-development problems. Compared with manufacturing or resource-based activities, services, by their nature, are seen as being more "footloose" and therefore easier to locate outside central regions and large urban areas. It is also argued that advances in telecommunications and computer technologies can further release many services from locational constraints.

Dynamic services, in particular, have attracted attention as a potential tool for stimulating the economies of regions suffering from slow development, for three reasons: they are growing rapidly; many of the jobs they generate are "good" jobs in terms of skill levels and incomes; and these services play a strategic role in investment, innovation, and technological change. By being a locus of competitive advantage, dynamic services can significantly influence the location of economic activity.

It turns out, however, that dynamic services, rather than being footloose, show quite concentrated locational patterns: they tend to be found in large cities. Table 3 shows employment concentration patterns for different industries in a sample of nine urban areas across the country in 1986. An index score greater than 100 for a town or city indicates that a given industry's labour force was disproportionately located in that area; a score of less than 100 indicates that the urban area had less than a proportionate share of that industry's labour force. The indices for dynamic services are directly related to the size of the urban centre. For these services, the degree of concentration is typically highest in the largest metropolitan areas. Note, for example, the high indices for finance, insurance, and real estate in Toronto, and for business services in Calgary, Toronto, and Vancouver. The role of Halifax as a regional centre of some importance is apparent; while the indices for the dynamic

Table 3

Index of Employment Concentration in Selected Cities and Towns, Dynamic Services,[1] 1986

	Toronto, Ont.	Montreal, Que.	Vancouver, B.C.	Calgary, Alta.	Halifax, N.S.	Kelowna, B.C.	Sault Ste. Marie, Ont.	Campbellton, N.B.	Matane, Que.
	(Thousands)								
Population	3,427	2,921	1,381	671	296	90	85	17	15
	(Canada = 100)								
Dynamic services	134	122	133	129	111	91	74	63	73
Transportation, communications, and utilities	97	117	130	111	116	80	87	92	96
Wholesale trade	136	122	123	112	100	93	69	66	59
Finance, insurance, and real estate	157	119	135	121	121	113	71	48	73
Business services	166	130	147	185	101	84	63	30	48

1 The index is measured as each industry's share of total employment in each city or town, as a proportion of that industry's share of total employment in Canada.
SOURCE Based on data from Statistics Canada.

services tend to be lower there than in the larger metropolitan areas, they are relatively high, compared with those of the smaller centres.

The pronounced concentration of dynamic services, which has been observed in other countries as well, suggests that they have very particular locational requirements. These include access to highly skilled labour, to complementary activities (such as office functions, financial institutions, and other services), and to a market (other businesses in the goods and service sectors). Large cities offer advantages with respect to all of those elements.

In fact, both dynamic-service firms and the head or divisional offices of major corporations tend to locate in large cities. Both are highly dependent upon access to information and face-to-face contact. As well, head offices depend increasingly upon the inputs of specialized service-sector firms in order to conduct their operations efficiently. On the other hand, branch plants, which are geographically more dispersed, have less need for producer services, since those services are, for the most part, provided through head offices; accordingly, branch plants create less demand for local service firms.

What, then, do these locational trends mean for regional development? First, the economic performance of the regions is becoming more strongly linked to the performance of their urban centres. Second, the potential for economic disparities *within* regions – between the largest cities and the smaller urban centres and rural areas – appears to be increasing. And third, disparities *between* regions are becoming more pronounced, since the major cities – the dominant centres of service growth – are disproportionately located in the developed regions.

Nonstandard Employment

"Nonstandard" work forms – those which differ from the traditional model of a full-time, full-year job – have increased their share of total employment in recent years. The most important of these is *part-time employment*, conventionally defined as including jobs with less than 30 working hours per week. Part-time work rose from 4 per cent of total employment in Canada in 1953 to 15 per cent by the mid-1980s; even as the labour market has tightened in recent years, the incidence of part-time employment has remained at that level. Since 1975, part-time work has accounted for at least 30 per cent of net job growth in every province except Alberta, Prince Edward Island, and Ontario; in Saskatchewan and Quebec, it has contributed over 40 per cent of the new jobs (Chart 5). Involuntary part-time employment – where workers would have preferred full-time jobs if they could have found them – has been increasing as well and now accounts for 24 per cent of all part-time employment. Nearly half of all part-time jobs created since 1981 have been classified as "involuntary" part-time.

Most part-time workers are employed in the traditional-service subsector, and the overwhelming majority are either

Chart 5

Contribution of Part-Time Employment to Total Employment Growth,[1] by Province, 1975-88

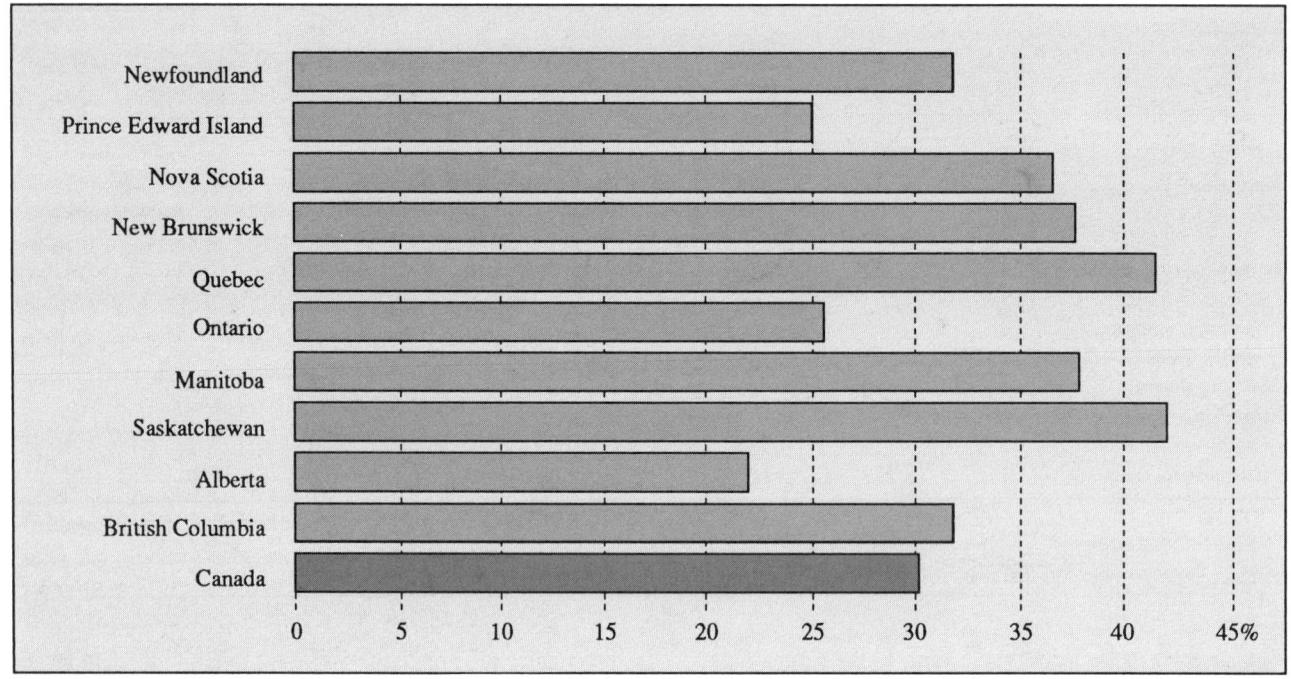

1 Estimated by dividing the difference in part-time employment between 1988 and 1975 by the difference in total employment over the same period.
SOURCE Based on data from Statistics Canada.

young or female (or both). By comparison with their full-time counterparts, part-time workers are much more likely to be short-term employees, to be nonunionized, and to be employed in very small firms. They are less likely to be covered by a range of employee benefits; and in general, they earn less, on an hourly basis, than full-time employees performing similar kinds of work.

Other forms of nonstandard employment are also growing. For example, the proportion of the employed labour force in *short-term work* (jobs of less than six months' duration) rose by nearly 2 percentage points between 1978 and 1988. By far the largest numbers of short-term jobs are found in traditional services. Most short-term workers are young; indeed, a significant number of them are full-time students. Short-term jobs are more likely than longer-term ones to be part-time and to be situated in small firms; they are less likely to be unionized or to be covered by a pension plan.

Another growing form of nonstandard work is *own-account self-employment*, which includes work by the self-employed who do not themselves have employees. During the past decade, 10 per cent of overall job growth has been in this category. The own-account self-employed are most frequently engaged in traditional services (chip-wagon operators, newsstand owners, one-truck movers, and so on). While there is a high degree of variability, their earnings tend to be lower than those of workers employed by others; in 1986, just over half of the self-employed earned less than $10,000, compared with 27 per cent of paid workers.

Temporary-help agency work has tripled in the 1980s and now stands at over 80,000. A 1988 survey of temporary-help workers found that 41 per cent were engaged in this type of employment because they could not find full-time jobs. Most temporary-help workers are in clerical occupations, and about 70 per cent are female. Wage levels are generally well below those for full-time workers, and fringe benefits are usually minimal.

Between 1981 and 1986, these four forms of nonstandard employment accounted for about half of all new jobs; they now represent nearly 30 per cent of total employment. Some of this increase can be attributed to the relatively slack labour markets of the 1980s. The future expansion of nonstandard employment may be curtailed, to some extent, by changes in the age structure of the work force. As Chart 6 indicates, total labour force growth has already begun to slow down, as Canada is now experiencing a significant decline in the inflow of young people into the labour market. Even when cyclical and demographic

Chart 6

Labour Force Growth, 1960-2000

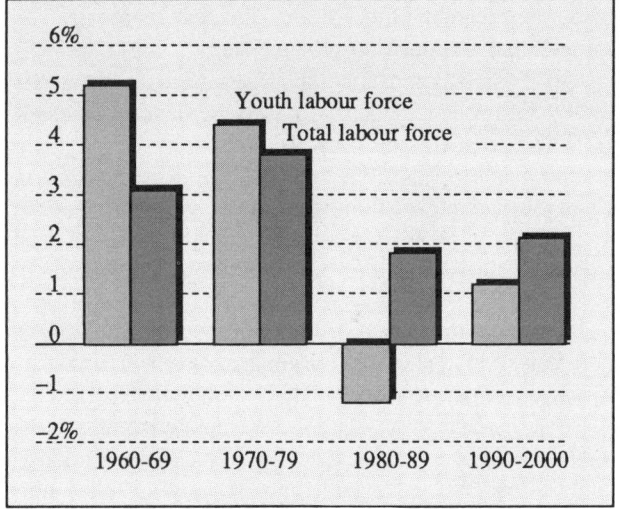

SOURCE Based on data from Statistics Canada and on projections by the Economic Council of Canada.

factors – and their implications for the availability of workers – are taken into account, however, our analysis indicates a long-term trend towards more nonstandard employment.

The growth in nonstandard employment forms cannot be simply attributed to the shift to services; these forms are concentrated within traditional services, but neither dynamic nor nonmarket services show high incidence rates (Chart 7). At the same time, nonstandard employment has also been growing in the goods sector. A more complete

Chart 7

Proportion of Workers in Nonstandard Employment, by Major Sector, 1986

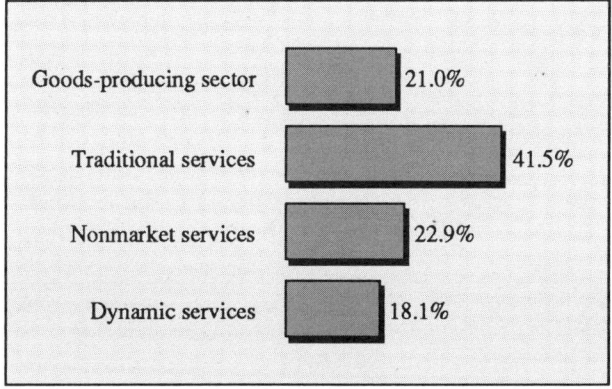

SOURCE Based on data from Statistics Canada.

explanation for the increase in nonstandard employment must recognize that part-time and short-term work is particularly prevalent in small firms and nonunion settings. And both small-firm and nonunion jobs, which are typical in both traditional and dynamic services, have represented major sources of employment growth during the 1980s.

The increase in nonstandard work has aroused a certain amount of controversy. To some analysts, it reflects the need for flexibility on the part of employers and workers. In opposition to this view, others contend that, while this development is serving the interests of employers, nonstandard jobs force workers to accept unstable employment, low pay, and minimal opportunities for training and promotion.

We recognize the benefits that nonstandard work forms offer employers in adjusting to changing market conditions. We also know that some people deliberately seek such jobs, for personal reasons. However, our analysis has shown that nonstandard workers generally earn less than others in full-time, more permanent jobs in the same occupations and the same industries and that, in the majority of cases, they have fewer fringe benefits. The earnings trends described later suggest that the increase in nonstandard jobs may be increasing the economic insecurity of growing numbers of workers.

Skill Trends

While "skill" is a difficult concept to measure, there is a growing body of research suggesting that the growth of services, technological innovation, and changes in the way work is organized are combining to transform both the nature and the level of the skills that are required in the labour market. Evidence from a series of service-industry case studies conducted by the Council indicates that the qualities that employers are now seeking include basic academic competence, creativity and initiative, analytical and problem-solving abilities, adaptability, and communication and interpersonal skills.

Certainly, one aspect of the changing skill profile is the growing emphasis on information-based work. According to our estimates, over half of Canadians are now employed in occupations that are primarily concerned with the creation and use of data and knowledge (Table 4). This information-based employment is especially prevalent in the service sector, where it accounts for nearly two thirds of all jobs; over the past 15 years, however, it has expanded rapidly in the goods sector as well. Indeed, on an economy-wide basis, such jobs accounted for two thirds of the net employment growth from 1971 to 1986.

Table 4

Information-Based Employment, 1971-86

	As a proportion of total employment		As a proportion of total employment growth
	1971	1986	1971-86
	(Per cent)		
Service sector	59.2	63.2	69.0
Goods sector	22.1	27.4	57.6
Both sectors	45.1	52.4	67.5

SOURCE Estimates by the Economic Council of Canada, based on census data from Statistics Canada.

Information-based employment can vary considerably in terms of the skills and education required. Jobs that involve the development and interpretation of information typically have a high knowledge content. On the other hand, where information work involves the routine production of data, skill levels are far lower.

Overall, the occupational shifts that have occurred over the past 15 years have led to an acceleration in the growth of highly skilled jobs – i.e., managerial, administrative, and professional and technical occupations. These categories accounted for one third of all employment growth from 1971 to 1981, and 77 per cent of the growth from 1981 to 1986. As a result, their share of total employment rose from 19 to 26 per cent over the period 1971-86. And according to the most recent projections of the federal government, they will account for over half of the net job creation over the next decade.

A major reason for the growth of these highly skilled occupations is their expanding share within all industries; however, this development can also be attributed, in part, to the employment shift towards the service sector. The occupational composition of some service industries – financial, business, and nonmarket services – is characterized by high skill and educational requirements in comparison with the goods sector. On the other hand, employment in traditional services tends to have lower skill levels. Even where jobs are information-based in this subsector, they are predominantly involved with the routine production of data; a disproportionate share of these jobs are held by women.

On balance, the skill distribution in the service sector is more polarized than that in the goods sector, which is characterized by intermediate-level skill requirements. Thus the employment shift to services is contributing to gains in the highly skilled occupations, a decline in the share of middle-level skilled jobs, and a stable proportion of low-skill jobs.

Earnings Trends

While Canadian workers enjoyed significant income gains during the late 1960s and early 1970s, real compensation peaked in 1977 and had actually declined slightly a decade later. A number of factors appear to have contributed to this stagnation in labour income, including the slowdown in productivity growth and a reduction in the bargaining power of workers. In the decade prior to 1977, real-wage increases surpassed productivity growth, but in the decade following that year, wages lagged behind gains in productivity.

As well, the earnings of Canadian workers have become more polarized over the past two decades. Table 5 sum-

Table 5

Median Earnings of the Labour Force[1] and Distribution by Earnings Level, 1967-86

	Median earnings	Earnings level[2]				Inequality index[3]
		Low	Middle	High	Total	
	(1986 dollars)	(Per cent)				
1967	15,088	36.4	26.8	36.9	100.0	0.39
1973	17,285	37.2	23.7	39.1	100.0	0.41
1981	18,046	38.2	23.4	38.3	100.0	0.40
1986	17,395	39.4	21.5	39.1	100.0	0.42

1 The labour force here consists of those workers whose earnings were at least 5 per cent of the average industrial wage.
2 Defined as follows: "low" – jobs with earnings ranging up to 75 per cent of the median; "middle" – jobs with earnings ranging between 75 and 125 per cent of the median; and "high" – jobs with earnings over 125 per cent of the median.
3 As measured by the Gini coefficient, which rises with the degree of inequality.
SOURCE Estimates by the Economic Council of Canada and by Statistics Canada, based on the Survey of Consumer Finances.

marizes the results of a study of income distribution trends undertaken jointly by the Economic Council and Statistics Canada. It shows that there has been an increase in the "Gini coefficient," which is the conventional index of inequality. And there has been a trend away from the middle, with the distribution having shifted to the high and low ends of the scale. In 1967, 27 per cent of the Canadian work force had annual earnings that we have categorized as "middle-level" – i.e., within 25 per cent of the median on either side. By 1986, only 22 per cent of the labour force fell within this group. This polarization has taken place in all regions of the country, with the decline of the middle-level group ranging from 4 percentage points in the Prairies to 8 points in Ontario. Nationally, and in most regions, the "declining middle" was accounted for by roughly equal shifts to the upper and lower groups.

The growing polarization in earnings applies to families as well (Table 6). However, when the distribution of *total* income (earnings plus income from investments and transfers) for families is considered, polarization is not as evident – at least not since 1973. These results suggest that nonemployment income (presumably in the form of transfers) is offsetting at least some of the increasing disparity in labour income. In the present context of large budgetary deficits and mounting public debt – and of pressures to contain public expenditures – it is troubling to consider that the transfer system could be facing an added redistributive challenge because of a growing disparity in incomes from work.

Table 6

Middle-Income Families, 1967-86

	Proportion of families with middle-level income[1]			
	1967	1973	1981	1986
	(Per cent)			
Income type				
Employment income	34.4	31.9	31.8	29.6
Total income (pre-tax)	26.1	22.5	23.1	22.3
Total income (post-tax)	..	25.1	25.8	25.0

1 Proportion of "census families" – i.e., families consisting of a husband and wife (with or without children who have never married), living together in the same dwelling – with income that is between 75 and 125 per cent of the median.
SOURCE Estimates by the Economic Council of Canada and by Statistics Canada, based on the Survey of Consumer Finances.

An important question is whether the growing earnings polarization is a permanent trend or whether it is self-correcting. The answer requires an understanding of the causes of this phenomenon – a difficult task, since there are many problems associated with identifying, disentangling, and measuring the various effects.

Essentially, there are two classes of potential explanations: one is concerned with the shifting composition of the labour force, while the other considers changes in the structure and operation of the economy. The first of these is based on the hypothesis that the increasing participation of women in the work force and the entry of the baby-boom generation into the labour market have depressed wages and skewed the distribution of incomes towards the low end of the scale. Our analysis suggests that changes in the composition of the labour force have indeed contributed to increased income disparity; this can only be a partial explanation, however, since earnings polarization can be observed in all age/sex groups, including prime-age males.

Have structural changes in the economy itself played a role in the increasing income disparity? It has been argued that the transition from goods to services has been accompanied by a shift from activities with earnings profiles concentrated at middle levels to activities in either high- or low-wage industries. In this regard, we have already noted that, on balance, the distribution of skills is more polarized in the service sector than in the goods sector. It is also true that the service industries that have contributed the most to overall employment growth have either very high average wages (health and social services) or very low ones (retail trade and personal services). This level of analysis, however, is only partial, since it does not consider patterns of earnings distributions *within* industries. Once this is taken into account, it becomes apparent that the shift towards services is not a major explanation for the growth in income disparity. Indeed, we have found that increased income polarization has occurred within all industry groupings, in the goods sector as well as the service sector.

The apparent pervasiveness of the polarization does suggest that the changes that are taking place in the workplace and within industries are fundamental and systemic. In this regard, we note that the trend towards wage polarization is at least as strong in the United States as it is in Canada. In that country, some observers have argued that economic globalization and technological innovation have resulted in raising the wages of highly skilled workers and depressing those of workers with lower skills. Others have stressed changes in human-resource management, including the growing use of nonstandard workers and the declining impact of unions on the wage-determination process.

16 Good Jobs, Bad Jobs

At this point, however, some part of the explanation continues to elude us. We do not know whether the polarization, observed over a relatively short period, is merely a one-time disturbance, whether it is the beginning of a new trend that will become more significant over time, or whether it will be reversed, at least to some extent, as the baby-boom generation moves into the prime-age, and presumably higher-wage, category.

Adjusting to the Changing Job Structure

As job opportunities are becoming increasingly concentrated in the service sector, it is apparent that changes in the nature of work go beyond a simple shift in the industry of employment. As we have seen, the transformation of the job structure also involves changes in the geographic location of work, the form of employment, skill requirements, and compensation. How well are Canadians adjusting to the new patterns of employment?

In considering the question of adjustment, the first thing to understand is that change is a constant. In any year, about one out of three workers experiences a spell of unemployment or a job change. In part, this "churning" reflects worker-initiated movements – e.g., those of voluntary job changers and of students moving in and out of the labour market. And in part, it reflects employer-initiated changes, as markets, production methods, and comparative advantages shift.

When workers lose or leave their jobs – in the economist's parlance, when they "separate" from their jobs – they typically try to find another within the same industry, where they have experience and where they are likely to have appropriate skills and good information about job vacancies. However, with new opportunities being increasingly concentrated in services, people leaving jobs in goods industries often must change sectors to find another position: in 1986, over 40 per cent of those separating from goods-industry employment found their next job in services.

There is considerable variation in how effectively workers are adapting to the changing employment patterns. Some people appear to be very mobile: in 1986, for example, about one quarter of those who separated from their jobs found new positions within four weeks (Chart 8). For many others, however, the adjustment to changes in the labour market seems difficult. Note that about one third of job changers had not found new employment 26 weeks later. Three groups stand out as having had particular problems: older workers, workers with low educational attainment, and people who have been laid off.

Chart 8

Distribution of Job Separators by the Number of Weeks of Joblessness, 1986

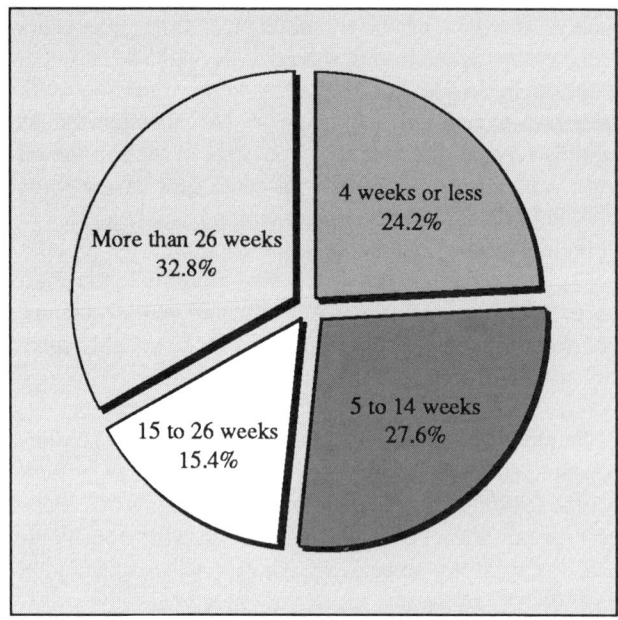

SOURCE Estimates by the Economic Council of Canada, based on data from Statistics Canada.

Older Workers

The labour market situation of older workers has deteriorated over the past decade. This is most evident when we look at the substantial increase in their long-term unemployment since the 1981-82 recession (Table 7). These data underline the immobility of older workers.

Table 7

Long-Term Unemployment,[1] by Age Group, 1981 and 1987

	1981	1987
	(Per cent)	
Age group		
15 to 24	3.0	4.1
25 to 44	5.2	10.0
45 and over	4.8	16.9
All age groups	4.5	9.4

1 The rates are based on the number of people in each age group who were continuously unemployed for 53 weeks or more, as a proportion of all unemployed workers in that age group.
SOURCE Based on Syed Sajjadur Rahman, Surendra Gera, and John Touchie, "Long-term unemployment: The Canadian experience," a paper prepared for the Economic Council of Canada, 1989.

Compared with those in younger age groups, older workers are less likely to have the education and skills needed for information-based employment; at the same time, they are less likely to take up nonstandard jobs. After separating from a job, older workers – particularly those aged 55 and over – have a considerably lower probability of finding another one than do workers in other age groups. While just under one third of all job changers in 1986 were still not re-employed six months later (see Chart 8), the corresponding figure was 54 per cent for job changers aged between 55 and 64.

Poorly Educated Workers

Workers with low levels of educational attainment have always experienced relative difficulty in the labour market. Moreover, as more and more employment becomes information-based, the employment problems facing the poorly educated appear to be growing. As Chart 9 indicates, the unemployment "hazard" associated with low levels of educational attainment increased considerably between 1975 and 1988.

Chart 9

Level of Schooling and Rate of Unemployment, 1975-88

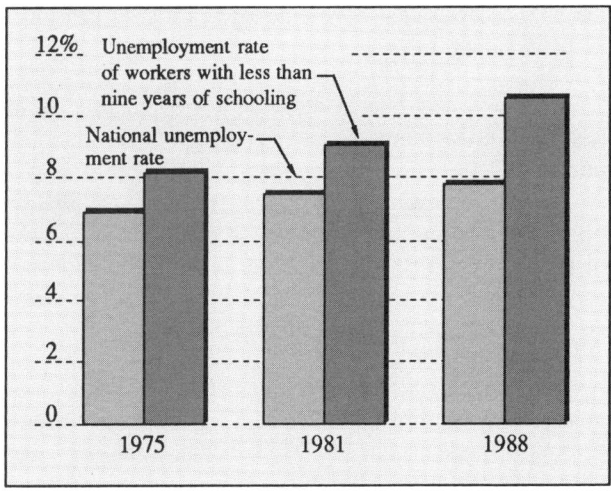

SOURCE Based on data from Statistics Canada.

Laid-Off Workers

People who lose their job tend to face much more difficult adjustments than those who quit, and the average time required to find a second job is more than twice as long for them. Laid-off individuals also face greater prospects of lower wages upon re-employment (Chart 10), regardless of whether their next job is in the same industry or in a different sector.

Chart 10

Job Changes and Wage Loss, 1986

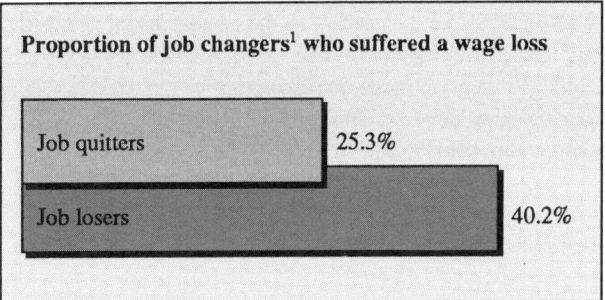

1 Includes only those job changers separating from their first job of 1986.
SOURCE Based on data from Statistics Canada.

Conclusion

The emerging job structure has a number of favourable elements. The most obvious has been the rate of employment creation since the 1981-82 recession, particularly in the nation's major cities, where the development of dynamic services has been impressive. Moreover, a significant portion of the growth has been in occupations that have a high skill content and offer very good compensation.

We are concerned, however, by some trends that, together, suggest a growing segmentation in the labour market. This is evident, for example, from our analysis of labour-adjustment patterns, which suggests that while part of the work force appears to be very mobile, other groups are experiencing difficulty in adapting to the changing job profile. We have also found evidence of segmentation in terms of earnings, skill content, job stability, and the location of employment. Two quite distinct "growth poles" account for virtually all of the employment expansion in the 1980s: one includes highly skilled, well-compensated, stable jobs, while the other consists of nonstandard jobs with relatively low levels of compensation and stability. The implication of our research is that the labour market is offering economic security to fewer Canadians.

Certainly, the expansion of the service sector has been a major factor in defining the emerging job structure; however, some of the most important trends are not limited to service industries. The changing nature of employment should be more properly seen as the result of a number of developments, including not only the growth of services but, also, technological innovation and the information explosion, economic globalization, and the changing composition of the work force. These factors, together, are transforming the labour market. Accordingly, as our attention turns to policy matters in the remainder of this Statement, our comments are not restricted to the service sector alone. Rather, we focus on a changing labour market where, among other developments, growing numbers of people are engaged in service activities.

Conclusions and Policy Implications

Our analysis suggests that the Canadian labour market in the 1990s will be defined by the following features:

– slow growth of the work force, with an older age profile;

– increasing employment in service activities;

– more work with high knowledge content;

– concentration of "good" jobs in large cities;

– growth of nonstandard employment forms; and, possibly,

– widening disparities in the quality of jobs and in the degree of economic security they provide for workers.

These changes are likely to have far-reaching consequences for all Canadians. They will shape the education and training decisions of young people and the career patterns of the adult work force. They will influence the roles and concerns of Canada's social institutions, from families to unions. And they will undoubtedly affect the approaches of industry to the management of human resources.

Our portrait of the emerging labour market also has important consequences for a wide range of public policies. The growth of services, along with the information explosion and the internationalization of business activity, is fuelling the demand for an increasingly well-educated and skilled work force. Canada's future economic welfare will be dictated in no small measure by its capacity to develop human resources. The "education-and-training" imperative will also be compelling for individuals, since employment experiences will be less and less favourable for those who have skill deficiencies. In fact, our analysis suggests that the segmentation of the labour market into "good-job" and "bad-job" sectors is likely to raise considerable challenges for policymakers concerned with the economic security of Canadians. Certainly, the presence of competitive industries is essential for a robust labour market that can pro-

vide that security. We have found that the quality and efficiency of service deliverers and their integration with goods producers is increasingly critical to this competitiveness; accordingly, economic development policies must recognize and support the role of services.

Labour market policies will have to adapt to these transformations; indeed, our research suggests that some institutions no longer "fit" the needs of Canadian workers and employers. In the pages that follow, we look at how policies might be reshaped to support job creation and to maximize the contribution of Canada's human resources in the changing environment. We reiterate here the three interrelated principles that should, in our view, underlie a strategy that recognizes the new dynamics of the labour market:

1 strengthen the commitment to the development of human resources;

2 promote economic security for workers; and

3 recognize the role of services in economic growth.

In making our recommendations, we are aware that actions taken today have implications for future generations. Indeed, that was the theme of the Council's Annual Review for 1989, entitled *Legacies*, which highlighted two elements – the capacity to develop Canada's human resources and the public debt – that have a direct bearing on the policy discussion that follows.

We believe that human-resource development is an investment in the future. Canada's success in the emerging information-based service economy will depend heavily on its capacity to develop a first-rate work force; and that capacity must be put in place now. In emphasizing the role of education and training, we note that a macroeconomic context that supports high rates of employment growth is an important condition for realizing that goal.

To some extent, however, Canada's human-resource objectives lie in direct conflict with the legacy of the public debt. Canada cannot achieve its labour force goals simply by digging deeper into the public purse. Accordingly, we have not made any recommendations that would increase government spending over the next several years. Rather, our suggestions are intended, in large part, to shift policy emphasis in order to better reflect the changing environment. Some of our proposals would, however, require new spending by the private sector, because there are areas where current efforts are inadequate.

In recent years, the Economic Council has drawn attention to the rapid changes in the economic environment and to their implications for Canadians. Generally, we have advocated adaptation to market forces as the best approach to meet the challenges of an increasingly competitive global economy; this has been our perspective in supporting trade liberalization, more-rapid adoption of new technologies, and less regulation in product markets. In advocating that approach, we recognize the growing pressure on the labour market, both to generate the skills that are so critical to competitiveness and to provide mechanisms for individuals to adjust to the accelerating changes they face. This perception has been reinforced by the research that we have undertaken for this Statement.

The Council believes that, as much as possible, the goals of human-resource development and labour adjustment should be achieved through the actions of employers, unions, and individual workers, responding to market forces. At the same time, however, there is an important role for governments in the functioning of labour markets and in cushioning the hardships inflicted on individuals. Public policies must work with market forces to strengthen the commitment to human resources and to promote the economic security of workers, thereby maximizing the contributions of all Canadians.

Strengthen the Commitment to the Development of Human Resources

The development of human resources contributes to competitiveness and employment growth, and it plays a significant part, as well, in achieving distributional objectives. While this has always been the case, a number of trends – including technological change, the information revolution, and the intensifying global competition – are combining to make human-resource development more critical than ever before.

Our research indicates that work with high-skill and educational requirements represents a growing share of overall employment. Many high-skill jobs in both the goods-producing industries and services are trade-sensitive, if not directly dependent on trade; as global competition accelerates, high-cost countries such as Canada will be forced to rely increasingly on the excellence of their work force to provide a comparative advantage in the global marketplace.

A growing number of jobs are information-based; even those which do not have a high-skill content demand basic literacy and numeracy. To gain employment – particularly, stable, well-compensated employment – people now need an adequate educational base. The unskilled and poorly educated are experiencing greater disadvantage in the labour market and, in particular, are facing special problems in adjusting to the changing employment structure.

While every country must invest in all factors of production – including capital and technology – the achievement of a high return on these investments will require people with the skills and knowledge to exploit their potential. Increasingly, then, the performance of national economies is closely linked to the human factor. To put it simply, Canadians should not expect to improve – or even maintain – their standard of living unless, as a nation, they attach a high priority to the quality of the work force. Thus effective education and training policies will be absolutely fundamental to Canada in the coming decades.

Human-resource development must be a major priority for policymakers. Accordingly, industry, labour, educators, and governments must aggressively pursue a human-resource strategy that will emphasize, on the one hand, a broadly based education system and, on the other, an active, industry-based training system, with the primary focus to be on the development of specific vocational skills.

Education

In terms of labour force preparation, Canada's education systems must meet two imperatives. The first is to ensure that basic levels of competency are universally held: all Canadians must have literacy and numeracy skills and, more generally, the analytical tools to "navigate" in an information-based society. The second imperative is to pursue a standard of excellence through the development of highly educated individuals. These two objectives involve all education levels, from primary to postsecondary.

The Economic Council is concerned about the performance of the Canadian education systems, when measured against such criteria. While recognizing that there have been some positive developments, we have noted a number of disturbing indicators that raise serious questions about the quality of education in this country:

• Close to one fifth of the adult population is functionally illiterate (reading at, or below, the Grade 9 level).

• A relatively high secondary-school dropout rate (nearly 30 per cent), coupled with a scarcity of apprenticeship and training programs, means that more young people fall outside the formal education and training system than is the case for many of Canada's competitors: only 72 per cent of Canadian 17-year-olds participate in a formal education or training program, compared with 87 per cent of Americans and 94 per cent of Japanese.

- Although Canada has a high rate of postsecondary attendance, some studies suggest that one reason for this is a relatively less demanding secondary curriculum than that of many other countries.

- Canada has failed to rank above the middle level in several international comparisons of student achievement in mathematics and science.

- A disturbingly high proportion of those taking trade and vocational programs do not appear to benefit from their education: graduates experience high unemployment rates and low average earnings, and the majority report that they do not use the skills acquired in their studies.

- By some international standards, the quality of the high-skill segment of the Canadian work force is only mediocre: according to the 1989 World Competitiveness Scoreboard, Canada ranks in the middle group with respect to managerial talent, research and development personnel, and skilled labour.

At first glance, these unsatisfactory "output" indicators do not seem to be the result of inadequate "inputs." Although real expenditure per student at the postsecondary level has declined over the past decade, spending on primary and secondary students has been rising steadily. Overall, Canada's public expenditures on education, as a percentage of gross domestic product, are the second highest among developed countries; indeed, this country's financial commitment to education rivals that of any other nation.

Our review of education performance has led us, then, to ask why Canada, as a nation, does not appear to be getting a greater economic return on its substantial investments in this area. Indeed, the growing public debate on education and the increased calls for some action suggest that this concern is becoming more widespread. Most recently, at the First Ministers' Conference in November 1989, the Prime Minister proposed that the provincial and federal governments create a working group to develop recommendations about how Canada's education systems might effectively respond to the human-resource requirements anticipated in the emerging economy.

By the time we completed the drafting of this Statement, we did not yet have full information on the scope of the Prime Minister's initiative or on how the provinces will respond. The usefulness of any policy dialogue on education and the future quality of Canada's workers will depend, however, on the availability of better empirical analysis. Hard and well-focused research is badly needed on how Canada's education systems can prepare a high-quality, competitive work force, capable of adapting to a rapidly changing knowledge-based economy.

Accordingly, we believe that a major empirical study into the state of education in Canada must be undertaken, with a view to evaluating concerns about the quality of education in this country. The focus of the study should be the link between education and economic goals – specifically the future competitiveness of Canada's work force in a knowledge-based economy. This is largely uncharted territory, raising formidable questions about concepts and measurements. It also brings to the fore sensitivities among educators, industry, and governments. Nonetheless, a stronger body of empirical research is bound to enhance the reform process within the various education systems across the country.

Training and Labour Adjustment

While high-quality education represents the essential precondition for a first-class work force, the development of vocational skills must be based in the training system. Training is essential for enhancing on-the-job performance and thus industrial competitiveness. It is also critical for facilitating labour adjustment. As changes in consumer demand and production methods accelerate, and as comparative advantages shift, the need for "retooling" is intensifying. The challenge for Canada's training system is to provide individuals with the ongoing opportunity to acquire productive skills that are needed in the marketplace.

As this Statement was being prepared, training and labour-adjustment policies were being reviewed by labour/management task forces, coordinated by the Canadian Labour Market and Productivity Centre at the request of the federal Minister of Employment and Immigration. While we look forward to the reports of these task forces, our own view is that the current training effort in this country is not satisfactory. It is beset by two major problems. First, the investment by Canadian industry in the development of human resources is insufficient; that situation is very unfortunate, especially in view of the substantial body of evidence showing that training is most effective when it is employment-based. Second, public policy continues to have a "damage-control" orientation, emphasizing income maintenance and short-term training for the long-term unemployed. Current programs do not offer adequate opportunities for developing skills that would improve real long-term employability.

Governments must play a dual role in this area if Canada is to develop the capacity for skill formation that we believe will be necessary in the future. First, they must provide training and adjustment opportunities for workers who are jobless, who face the prospect of unemployment, or who do not have a strong "attachment" to a particular employer. Second, governments must consider ways of stimulating the development of human resources within industry.

Policies Aimed at "Unattached" Workers

The conventional view of the labour market has been that individuals would work for the same employer for extended periods of time and that breaks in that relationship would be infrequent and would typically be associated with "cyclical" unemployment resulting from business downturns. That image of the labour market has been transformed, however, partly because of persistently high unemployment rates, partly because of the accelerating pace of economic change, and partly because of the proliferation of nonstandard employment forms. A growing proportion of the labour force has no attachment, or only a weak attachment, to a particular employer. Thus it will become more important in the 1990s for public policy to deal directly with those "unattached" workers, many of whom experience substantial economic insecurity. As well, the slowdown in the growth of the labour force will heighten the need to ensure that all Canadian workers can participate productively in the labour market.

In relative terms, Canada's level of public expenditure on labour market programs is comparable to that of the major countries of Western Europe and well above the U.S. and Japanese levels (Table 8). More than most, however, Canadian public policy has emphasized short-term income maintenance and not "active" strategies aimed at supporting workers in the acquisition of long-term employability; as the table shows, 75 per cent of Canadian spending on labour market programs in 1987 was allocated to income maintenance, mostly under the Unemployment Insurance Act.

Income maintenance through a traditional unemployment insurance (UI) system has an important adjustment role in providing earnings replacement in cases where unemployment is cyclical or seasonal or where some time is needed to locate a job opening. As this Council emphasized in its Annual Review for 1988, however, in the present context of rapid industrial and technological change, skill obsolescence, and growing regional imbalances, a large – and growing – proportion of unemployment is "structural" in nature. As a consequence, training, mobility, and counsel-

Table 8

Public Expenditure on Labour Market Programs, Selected Countries, 1987

	As a proportion of GDP	Proportion devoted to income maintenance[1]
	(Per cent)	
Canada	2.2	75.0
France (1986)	3.1	75.8
West Germany	2.3	57.7
Italy	1.3	63.8
Japan	0.6	71.2
Sweden	2.7	30.1
United Kingdom	2.6	65.4
United States	0.8	71.1

1 Including unemployment compensation and early retirement for labour market reasons (i.e., because the person is out of work or because his/her job has been released to the benefit of another person).
SOURCE Based on data from the Organisation for Economic Co-operation and Development.

ling services need to play a much larger role. The Council believes that public policy in this country must reflect the emerging labour market by more appropriately addressing the changing nature of labour adjustment; this does not necessarily require additional funding but rather a shift in emphasis towards a more active orientation. As a consequence,

1   **We recommend that reform of the federal government's labour market strategy move in the direction of supporting skill development and employability as the primary objective. As a long-run goal, we endorse a transition from the existing unemployment insurance fund to an "employment insurance" fund.**

The intention of this recommendation is to set out a broadly defined policy target. As we envisage it, the "employment insurance" (EI) fund would not be added to the UI fund but, rather, would be the end-product of a gradual transformation of the existing scheme into one that can more appropriately address the adjustment needs of Canadians. Unemployed workers could draw on the EI plan for income support in the event of unemployment (as is generally the case now); in addition, these workers would be able to use the fund for such purposes as skill development, mobility, and counselling. The actual form of the benefit would be determined by the insured worker, in consultation with Employment Centre counsellors, and it would depend on the individual's situation and on labour market conditions. If, for example, an unemployed worker had employable skills and if the period of joblessness were clearly temporary, income maintenance would be the appropriate approach; however, where immediate employment prospects were poor, benefits could be used for training or one of the other "active" measures.

The nature of the Canadian labour market now demands an adjustment strategy that will offer a range of options to unemployed workers – to receive straight income support, to improve employability, or to pursue some combination of the two. This imperative underlies our proposal for an EI fund.

Without dealing here with all of the specific design issues, many of the basic administrative principles of the existing UI system do seem to suit the needs of the new adjustment instrument we are calling for – e.g., benefit eligibility and benefit levels tied to the length of employment, as well as joint employee/employer contributions. These features could be preserved in the proposed EI scheme.

While we do not intend to set out the detailed fiscal arrangements that the proposed EI fund should entail, we would like to briefly discuss two financing aspects: first, the responsibilities of workers, employers, and government; and second, the overall funding levels that would be required. Regarding the former, the fund would involve both employee/employer contributions and public financing. While the financing responsibilities would have to be negotiated, in principle, government contributions should cover initiatives under the EI fund that are perceived to have "social" benefits for all Canadians; these would involve the "active" options of the fund and would include, for example, the direct costs of training and counselling expenses. On the other hand, employee/employer contributions should be applied principally towards the income-maintenance component of the fund. Undoubtedly, some expenses would fall into a "gray" area, and their financing would require both study and negotiation.

What would be the overall cost implications of the EI proposal? To the extent that the "active" options were pursued, the transition to the EI fund would likely imply higher costs, at least in the short run, than in a system where benefits are predominantly taken in the form of straight income maintenance, as is the case under the current UI system. Clearly, some of the incremental costs could be met through transfers of appropriate parts of the budget for the Canadian Jobs Strategy. If, however, the take-up rates for the active options were very high, thereby creating cost pressures on the fund, and if the current fiscal restrictions on the federal government remained, it might be necessary to limit the amount of financial support available under the active options.

Ultimately, we believe that by more effectively addressing labour adjustment through the principle of promoting employability, an EI fund would result in net savings through lower adjustment costs and a more productive work force.

As well, it is important to recognize that we are proposing that a labour market policy built on this sort of approach be implemented gradually. In that regard, an important transition step would be to increase the scope for the unemployed to acquire training while collecting UI benefits. Although Section 26 of the Unemployment Insurance Act does allow for retraining in some circumstances, training activity represents a minor part of the overall UI system, primarily because the share of UI funds allocated to Section 26 remains relatively small and because there have been substantial restrictions regarding eligibility and the choice of courses.

2   **We strongly support the principle of greater accessibility of training for the recipients of unemployment insurance benefits. Accordingly, we recommend that the federal government increase the UI funds available for retraining and relax the eligibility restrictions for training under the UI program.**

In making this recommendation, we support the proposal, made by the federal government in its April 1989 discussion paper on employment policy (entitled *Success in the Works*), to increase substantially the UI-fund allocations to training UI recipients under Section 26. We believe that the structure of the UI program – namely, the individual accounts and the contributory nature – is an appropriate one for supporting skill development. Indeed, this lies behind our vision of an EI fund. However, we do have reservations about another proposal in that document, aimed at reallocating additional UI funds, built up through universal employer/employee contributions, to programs outside the UI system that are not universally available. While we believe that UI claimants should have far greater access to training, their contributions should not be financing the expansion of federal labour market programs that are not necessarily targetted to the adjustment of unemployed workers.

We turn now to more selective policies for those categories of workers experiencing special problems in adapting to the changing employment structure. Two groups that are of particular concern are older workers and workers who have been laid off. Reintegrating those individuals into productive employment should be an important policy objective, particularly as Canada moves into an era of slow work-force growth, where changing patterns of employment cannot be met by relying on new entrants.

In this country, the conventional public-policy approach regarding older workers has been to compensate them for loss of employment. This philosophy underlies the Program for Older Worker Adjustment (POWA) – currently the major initiative in this area – which provides for compensation for permanently laid-off older workers. In a 1987 report, *Managing Adjustment*, which was released shortly after POWA had been announced, the Economic Council supported the notion of a program specifically concerned with the adjustment difficulties of older workers. Since then, we have undertaken more research on older-worker adjustment and POWA. Our findings have raised concerns about certain features of POWA, including its limited and somewhat subjective eligibility conditions.

A more fundamental concern, however, stems from our belief that the approach to older-worker adjustment should be centred on a positive reintegration strategy that emphasizes retraining and job-search counselling. Compensation programs like POWA are expensive and, by necessity, have very restricted coverage. Moreover, they do not adequately recognize the principle that productive employment is a key to full participation in our society. As Canada's work force continues to grow more slowly, the contribution of older workers to the economy will become more critical. Canada simply must learn to use its older workers effectively.

Certainly, the adjustment difficulties faced by these workers should not be minimized. Some are understandably reluctant to change jobs or careers, both for personal reasons and because the benefits they have built up may be jeopardized; with respect to the latter consideration, enhancing the portability of benefit plans is clearly an important objective. There is also a general reluctance, on the part of employers, to hire older people; this attitude is bound to change in the future, however, as employers will increasingly come to realize that older workers must be the solution for the labour shortages that they will face.

On balance, the Council finds that there are strong arguments supporting a policy strategy primarily aimed at reintegration rather than compensation. As well, some experiments with a focus on assisting older workers to acquire new employment skills suggest that reintegration is a viable approach to adjustment. We note, for example, the demand for the Transitions program in Ontario, which provides vouchers to institutions or employers offering training to individuals aged 45 years or more.

3 **We strongly endorse the principle of reintegration as the cornerstone of adjustment policy for older Canadians. In this regard, we recommend that publicly funded programs for these workers emphasize retraining and employment counselling.**

The reintegration principle is also important in the case of laid-off workers. We have noted the adjustment difficulties of these workers with respect to the length of time needed to find another job and to the frequency with which they experience wage cuts. Research indicates that re-employment outcomes are much more favourable when workers are informed in advance that they will be laid off. Adjustment is also assisted when labour and management work together to develop redeployment solutions for the employees affected.

Canadian jurisdictions currently have some minimum standards for providing advance notice to laid-off workers. While notice-period requirements vary considerably, in general they depend on either the employee's length of service or the number of workers who are being laid off. In the event of group layoffs, some jurisdictions also include positive redeployment measures, such as the advance provision of the profile of laid-off employees to the government or the creation of a firm-level adjustment committee.

The report of the federal government's Advisory Council on Adjustment – the de Grandpré Council – which was published in 1989, recommended minimum national standards regarding the advance notice of layoffs. The length of notice provided by the employer would depend on the number of workers involved in the layoff: two weeks would be required when fewer than five employees were to be laid off, with the notice period increasing in stages – up to 16 weeks when the layoff included 50 or more. Advance notice would be given to full-time and "regular" part-time workers; in the case of group layoffs, the employer would be required to provide the appropriate government with a profile of the affected employees and with a proposed compensation and redeployment package.

4 **We recommend that the federal, provincial, and territorial governments implement the national minimum advance-notice standards suggested by the de Grandpré report. The minimum notice period should be two weeks in the case of layoffs involving between one and four persons, four weeks where between five and nine persons are to be laid off, eight weeks where 10 to 49 persons are to be laid off, and 16 weeks in the case of layoffs of 50 people or more.**

The principle of this recommendation – that advance-notice requirements should depend on the magnitude of the layoff – reflects the fact that the adjustment problem tends to increase with the number of workers involved. In the event of a major layoff, large numbers of workers with similar skills and experience must search for new jobs at one point in time, frequently in industries and localities where job opportunities are relatively scarce. As a consequence, the challenges of a major layoff often can require more than advance notice.

In these situations, the re-employment possibilities of those who have lost their jobs may benefit significantly from adjustment plans developed at the firm level. These plans, typically developed by representatives of management and labour, address issues such as the skill profile of the laid-off workers, likely re-employment prospects, and appropriate counselling, mobility, and retraining options. While the government involved acts as a facilitator, provides information on labour market conditions and programs, and covers the administrative costs of the committee, it is the parties themselves that must work out a solution. As this Council has noted before, labour/management adjustment committees coordinated by the federal Industrial Adjustment Service (IAS) have a very positive and cost-effective record in layoff situations with respect to the re-employment of laid-off workers and the post-layoff climate within the firm itself; indeed, in two recent Statements, *Making Technology Work* and *Managing Adjustment*, we have expressed our strong support for the IAS committees.

Currently, industrial adjustment committees are required in the federal jurisdiction in the case of major layoffs (involving 50 or more workers); Quebec, Ontario, and Manitoba provide for the establishment of such committees at the request of the Minister of Labour. In practice, a high degree of flexibility exists in the application of this employment standard. In the federal jurisdiction, for example, the requirement for a committee is waived where the parties have established their own adjustment arrangement or where it would be a real burden, such as in a bankruptcy situation.

5   **We recommend that all jurisdictions establish a labour standard providing for the creation of a committee that will include management and labour representatives, to develop and implement a re-employment package for laid-off workers involved in a major layoff.**

Without identifying a precise definition of what constitutes a "major" layoff, we note that the most prevalent standard in Canadian jurisdictions is a loss of jobs for 50 workers or more.

The requirements set out in the two preceding recommendations are intended for situations where workers must seek new employment opportunities; they would not apply in cases where layoffs are seasonal or short-term in nature. In light of accelerating economic change, the re-employment problems faced by laid-off workers, and the observed benefits of advance-notice and adjustment committees, we believe that these proposals, which would clearly strengthen existing standards in most jurisdictions, would contribute to smoother adjustment in the Canadian labour market without imposing undue demands on employers.

Employer-Based Human-Resource Development

It is the Council's position that the overwhelming responsibility for job-related skill formation rests with business and labour. Indeed, the role of the private sector in human-resource development is crucial. We have already emphasized that employer-based training is the most effective approach for developing vocational skills and that, increasingly, human-resource development within industry is essential to Canada's competitiveness.

Ideally, a strong "training culture" should be created by forces operating at the firm level – by employers viewing skill formation as an essential element of human-resource management, by unions making training a priority, and by employees taking initiative to update existing skills and to acquire new ones. Certainly, there are examples of Canadian firms where this commitment to training by all parties exists. However, the information that is available suggests that the extent of private-sector training in this country is inadequate in a number of ways:

• Canadian employers appear not to train as much as their counterparts in many other industrialized nations; for example, according to preliminary data from a Statistics Canada survey, employer-sponsored training expenditures per worker in Canada are less than half the level observed in the United States.

• While some firms – generally large corporations – carry out a significant amount of training, Statistics Canada data suggest that most Canadian businesses provide no formal training at all (i.e., no skills development, carried out on the job or off-site, that has an identifiable plan and structure). The lack of training is most evident in small firms (fewer than 20 employees); however, even among medium-sized firms (20 to 200 employees), about one half report no training activities.

• Where employer-sponsored training is provided, it is heavily concentrated among highly skilled, well-educated male workers: the rest of the work force has far less access, particularly to comprehensive training opportunities.

These findings suggest that, overall, Canadian employers and employees need to make a much stronger commitment to training. This raises the question of what kinds of instruments might be effectively used to stimulate human-resource development at the level of the firm. There are a variety of "training triggers" that could be considered, including earned time off for training, employer-sponsored educational leave, and firm-level training trust funds. The most frequently discussed triggers are the grant-and-levy scheme and other tax-based arrangements. While there are a number of possible designs, a "training tax" would involve the imposition of an earmarked corporate tax that is refunded to firms up to the full amount, depending on the extent of training provided. This would create a financial incentive for firms to provide training at the same time as it would generate a pool of funds to finance training to fill gaps in the employer-sponsored effort.

Indeed, Canada's apparent "training gap" and a growing awareness of the harm that it can potentially inflict on this country in a globally competitive, information-based economy have led to increased calls for some kind of universally applied policy intervention to stimulate skill formation throughout the private sector. The credibility of this position as a serious option was established by a recommendation of the de Grandpré report for a training levy.

After reviewing training taxes and other types of triggers, however, we would not recommend the institution of a universally applied standard at this time. Any across-the-board intervention would need to be based on a number of principles: a simple administrative format; no new spending by governments; recognition of differences in training incentives for firms of different sizes and in different industries; access to training for all employees; a flexible definition of "training" that would extend beyond the traditional notion of formal courses; and no additional costs for firms already meeting the agreed-upon standards. Clearly, these requirements pose substantial design problems that could not be solved easily.

While ruling out the use of a universal instrument to stimulate training, we believe that a commitment to training could, in some industries where business and labour recognize that more skills formation is needed, be effectively created by planning at the sector level. We have noted some recent initiatives where employers and workers, together, identify skill needs in their industry and develop and implement an appropriate training plan. Sectoral initiatives can take on a variety of forms, depending on the nature of the industry, its organization, and its key human-resource issues. These approaches are not meant to replace but, rather, to encourage firm-level training plans.

Where there is no existing tradition of human-resource development, the Council sees considerable potential in sectoral approaches; while our remarks here focus on sector-based plans, we also note the effectiveness of some initiatives operating at the regional or local level.

The electrical-product and automotive-repair sectors are examples of industries that have created committees, involving both labour and management, that are charged with identifying and addressing sectoral human-resource issues. In some respects, the example of the automotive-repair scheme is of particular interest. That industry, like many of the growing service industries, is dominated by small firms and does not have well-established formal organizations on either the employer or the labour side. While, at first glance, these characteristics would not seem to be amenable to a sectorwide initiative, the automotive-repair experience demonstrates that a fragmented industry can be coordinated. Indeed, there may be a particular need for sector-based plans in industries of this type, which typically do not have a strong training record at the firm-level.

While a sector-based human-resource approach may not be suitable for all industries – and indeed may be redundant in industries with an established training record – we believe that these initiatives have a number of attributes that could make them interesting for sectors that do not have a strong tradition in this area. First and foremost, they can promote the private-sector responsibility that we see as being so critical. As well, there are advantages associated with being close to the scene, in terms of diagnosing the real problems and identifying tailor-made responses. Furthermore, these approaches offer a forum for labour and management to work together – and that, in itself, is a virtue.

Ultimately, business and labour in any industry must determine whether a sectoral training plan is appropriate; where it is, the initiative must come from the industry itself, with respect to both the commitment and the resources. Government can make a significant contribution simply by facilitating the creation of the industry committee and the development of its priorities. The Industrial Adjustment Service, for example, played a key role in the start-up of the electrical-product and automotive-repair initiatives. However, the ability of the IAS to support the creation of other industry-level plans is restricted by the relatively limited funds available for this purpose ($1 million in 1988-89).

6 **We encourage the provincial and federal governments to facilitate the emerging trend towards sector-based human-resource development initiatives. To this end,**

we recommend that the federal government allocate increased funds to the Industrial Adjustment Service to be used as "seed money" for the development of sector-specific human-resource plans in industries that have chosen to initiate such plans.

The Council believes that the level of skills development in Canadian industry is an issue of national concern. In our view, more active employer-based training represents a major challenge. The necessary investment in human resources should be generated by employers responding more realistically to the needs of the marketplace, by unions more frequently placing training issues on the bargaining table, and, in some instances, by industry-based human-resource committees implementing training plans more aggressively. One way or the other, training must become a fundamental activity for Canadian employers and a fundamental right for Canadian workers. Tomorrow's economy will require nothing less.

Promote Economic Security for Workers

The research undertaken for this Statement suggests that employment is becoming increasingly polarized into two categories – good jobs and bad jobs. This is most apparent when we look at trends in the distribution of employment income: over the past two decades, there has been a notable decline in the share of the work force with middle-level earnings. At the same time, the growth in nonstandard employment forms is leading to the emergence of a related dichotomy within the labour force: workers with well-paid, relatively stable jobs and with extensive legal protections; and workers in employment forms that are often more tenuous, usually less well-compensated, and nearly always less protected.

This polarization raises policy dilemmas in the prevailing context of restraint, since it appears to have increased the redistributive task facing the transfer system. It is difficult to determine an appropriate response to the evidence on income distribution, as it is not yet fully clear what factors underlie the observed polarization and whether it is a transitory or permanent phenomenon. We do believe, however, that employment must be the fundamental source of economic security in Canada; the capacity of the labour market to meet the economic-security needs of workers should therefore be strengthened.

The suggestions that we have made with respect to training should contribute to the economic security of workers. While training is not a panacea, many individuals experiencing difficulties in the labour market are severely constrained by a lack of education or by limited access to training. Improvements in those areas can substantially raise their prospects for upward mobility.

We believe, also, that stronger policies to protect nonstandard workers represent an important means of addressing some of the causes of the growing earnings inequality, since many low-income workers occupy those kinds of jobs. In coming to this conclusion, we have been struck by the complex nature of nonstandard employment and by the tensions involved in applying labour policies to those work forms.

Traditionally, employment standards and benefit programs were designed to fit stereotyped images of an average worker – typically a full-time male employed in the goods sector. While there has been progress, some regulations and benefits still afford a lesser degree of protection or coverage to certain groups of nonstandard workers.

Should employment standards and benefits be further extended to offer wider coverage to workers in nonstandard jobs? We are aware that there are strong arguments in opposition to this course of action. Some nonstandard workers are most concerned with their immediate cash flow – e.g., those with income problems and those who have only a casual attachment to the labour force. To the extent that improved security and benefits will result in less take-home pay, the short-run interests of these individuals will not be served by stronger policies in support of nonstandard employees. Another effect might well be to create disincentives to hire workers in nonstandard job forms, thereby reducing employment options for many workers and diminishing the operational flexibility of employers.

Although these arguments are valid, the Council ultimately supports the principle that nonstandard workers with an ongoing attachment to the labour force should not be excluded from the protections and benefits offered to those in full-time, more permanent jobs. The notion of labour force attachment has changed, and policies to support the working population must keep pace. Moreover, many workers are involuntarily in nonstandard jobs and would prefer full-time, full-year positions if they could find them. Our concern, here, is heightened by the fact that the incomes, benefits, and job security of workers in nonstandard jobs are generally lower than for people doing similar types of work in more conventional employment forms.

Our analysis does lead us to the conclusion that the recent growth of nonstandard employment is part of a long-term trend. If that is indeed the case, steps must be taken to ensure that nonstandard work will offer more benefits and greater protection. This may well have social consequences too; indeed, we have noted the growing frequency of labour disputes where the central issue for labour is security.

Policymakers must bear in mind the new employment diversity and explicitly address the situation of workers in the new employment forms. In doing so, they face the dilemma of providing the intended support to nonstandard employees without undermining the flexibility needs of these workers or of employers.

Employment Standards

Some of the current employment standards should be extended to certain nonstandard employment forms. The case is perhaps most compelling with respect to part-time workers, specifically those who develop a continuous and regular relationship with an employer. Indeed, part-time employees often have an attachment to their employer and to the labour market that is comparable to that of full-time employees. For example, some individuals (often those with household responsibilities) enter into an explicit arrangement with an employer to work part-time on a continuing basis; for some other part-time workers, an ongoing relationship with a particular employer develops over time. We believe, partly on grounds of equity, that part-time employees who develop such ongoing relationships with employers should be entitled to receive the same benefits, pro-rated, as full-time workers. And beyond considerations of fairness, access to employee benefits is an important step in improving the prospects of many workers, very frequently women, for achieving economic security through employment. Many of those benefits, from pensions to various types of insurance, have the effect of reducing the number of people who need the safety nets provided by public benefit programs. Accordingly,

7   **We support the adoption of legislation in all jurisdictions that will provide for the inclusion of part-time employees with an on-going employer attachment, on a pro-rated basis, in all employee-benefit programs normally available to full-time employees.**

Although we have provided above a couple of general examples of what we mean by an "ongoing employer attachment," we recognize that they constitute less than a complete definition. Developing such a definition is an appropriate subject for consultation among the groups affected.

Public Benefit Programs

The economic security of nonstandard workers would also be favourably affected by ensuring that they are not unreasonably excluded from public benefit programs. Here, too, policymakers must recognize that the nature of labour force attachment – the "litmus test" for coverage – is changing.

8   **As a general principle, we urge that awareness of the new employment diversity be incorporated into the design of public benefit programs, with a view to ensuring that workers in nonstandard employment forms are not excluded from these benefits.**

To offer one example, the unemployment insurance system has traditionally determined eligibility for benefits, in part, on the basis of labour force attachment; in some ways, however, the criteria used to establish the degree of attachment have not kept pace with changing labour market realities. At present, in order to qualify for benefits, employees must earn at least 20 per cent of the UI earnings ceiling or work 15 or more hours per week, for a specified number of weeks depending on their geographical location. As a result, a part-time employee may be ineligible even though he/she may have accumulated more hours of employment than, for instance, a full-time employee with the minimum number of weeks of employment.

Pensions

Relative to the working-age population, the economic status of Canadians aged 65 and over has improved substantially over the past two decades. And undoubtedly, they will benefit in the future as a result of improvements during the 1980s in pension-standards legislation in jurisdictions that cover 80 per cent of the Canadian labour force. Benefits, protection, and portability will continue to be enhanced for those who are members of pension plans. As well, a larger proportion of the labour force has purchased registered retirement savings plans (RRSPs).

Pension reform has not helped those who are not covered by a work-related plan, however. And it is important to note that the proportion of the work force taking part in employer pension plans has been declining – from 40 to 37 per cent between 1980 and 1986. The locus of employment growth in the 1980s – largely in nonstandard employment forms and in small firms – is very likely to have contributed to this decrease. We know, for example, that pension coverage is only about 15 per cent both among part-time workers and among workers employed in firms with fewer than 20 employees.

This recent decline in work-related pension coverage gives cause for concern. The design of Canada's public pension system (which includes Old Age Security, the

Guaranteed Income Supplement, and the Canada and Quebec Pension Plans) is effectively predicated on the premise that Canadians will acquire private-pension entitlements throughout their working lives. If the trends observed during the 1980s persist, however, they may call into question the validity of that assumption. In light of these considerations,

9 We urge governments to evaluate on an ongoing basis the adequacy of Canada's combined private and public pension systems. Governments should be alert to the possibility that labour market trends may necessitate further rethinking of the overall approach to retirement income security in the 1990s.

Recognize the Role of Services in Economic Growth

While the main focus of our research has been on labour market policy, our study has led us to recognize that the shift to services also has profound implications for economic development. Although specific recommendations in that area are beyond the scope of this Statement, we suggest general directions for economic development policies, in light of the changing contribution of services to economic growth.

A strong conclusion of our examination of the growth of the service economy is that a successful economic strategy must not only reinforce the importance of both resources and manufacturing industries, but must also recognize the contribution of services to overall economic growth. Service industries are important sources of employment and output. Competitiveness and productivity growth are key to an economy in which more and more people are working in services, especially since services are becoming increasingly internationalized.

The efficiency and the quality of the service industries themselves must become a key focus of economic development policy. Policies that identify and foster linkages between goods and service producers, and that improve the quality and effectiveness of those linkages, should be encouraged.

Industrial Policy

Historically, Canadian industrial policy has focused on the resource and manufacturing sectors. Eligibility requirements for access to government grant, subsidy, and tax-relief programs have tended to apply to capital investments in plant and equipment for the production of goods. As the efficiency and quality of the service sector become increasingly important to overall living standards, however, those biases must be eliminated. Governments must become explicitly aware of the unintended "steering effects" built into policies and programs that were designed for a goods-based economy. Public policy that focuses on general economic development should, in fact, be neutral in its treatment of goods and services.

One important example of the bias towards goods producers involves technology policy. Innovation and technological change are fundamental to productivity growth and competitiveness in both goods and service industries. Canadian policy in this area, however, focuses on the development of new technologies by the goods industries. Little research has been done on how the processes of innovation and diffusion take place in the service sector, although some pioneering work suggests that service-sector innovation patterns may be quite different from those in the goods sector. Innovation in the service sector does not come from scientists working in laboratories, for example, but rather involves new ways of organizing and delivering services. Accordingly,

10 We urge governments to review their overall policy stance towards innovation and the service sector. They should discuss these issues with the appropriate industry associations and with experts in the field, for the purpose of developing an innovation policy that would reflect the contribution of R&D and technological change to economic growth in services.

Some key questions need to be answered: How does the pace of innovation among Canadian service producers compare with that of their counterparts elsewhere? Are there identifiable problems in the process of innovation diffusion? If so, what actions could be taken by industry and governments? Are some service producers more in need than others of policy support to improve their innovation performance?

Innovation represents just one example of non-neutrality in industrial policy. Industry, Science and Technology Canada (ISTC) is now undertaking a series of consultations with other federal departments to determine the degree to which anti-service-sector biases are built into a range of policies and programs. This effort is essential, in our view, and we urge all departments to regard this review as being of the utmost importance.

Linking Goods and Services

An important emphasis of industrial policy should be on facilitating linkages between goods and service industries.

Some programs recently initiated by ISTC incorporate that emphasis. A good example of this type of approach is a program developed by the Canadian Textiles Institute, the Canadian Apparel Manufacturers Institute, and the Retail Council of Canada in cooperation with ISTC. The Canadian Manufacturers and Retailers Council (CANMARC) provides a centralized source of specialized information to assist manufacturers and retailers in the coordinated use of technologies such as bar-coding and electronic data interchange.

CANMARC has only recently been established, and it remains to be seen whether its efforts will be successful. In our view, however, it has many attractive features: its purpose is to facilitate industry linkages; its development heavily involved the private sector; and the industries that joined together traditionally have lagged in the introduction of new technologies.

Other industries could benefit from similar types of arrangements; indeed, interest has been expressed by some of them. CANMARC-type programs could be especially useful in regions with a resource-based economy; those regions which are based on agriculture or fishing, in particular, face difficult problems in fostering linkages between sectors, since awareness and use of both the services themselves and of the technologies so important for linkages are relatively low in those industries.

11 We urge industry associations and governments to work together to develop programs that contain "linkage" features, such as those of CANMARC, for other groups of industries that are connected through customer/supplier relationships. Furthermore, we recommend that an early emphasis be placed upon involving resource producers.

Government's role in the development of such programs should be to act as facilitator, bringing complementary industries together to develop cooperative arrangements. No new public spending commitments are implied.

Service Infrastructure

Given the largely intangible nature of service outputs, the key elements of that sector's infrastructure are telecommunications and computer technology: these are the "highways" that "transport" those "products" nationally and internationally. A nation or region that lacks an up-to-date infrastructure will lag behind others in attracting and developing dynamic services; not only will job opportunities in services suffer, but – given the synergies – the goods sector will be adversely affected as well. Traditional services (notably, retail trade) are also critical components in an interdependent economy, since they represent the final contact between the commercial marketplace and the producers of consumer products. Consequently, the infrastructure linking producers and consumers through retailers must also be a priority.

Canada's telecommunications system is among the most technologically sophisticated in the world. It has the potential to provide Canadian industry with a comparative advantage in the current shift to information-intensive activities. That potential can only be fully realized, however, if a conscious effort is made to shape the telecommunications infrastructure so that it will help to foster the establishment and growth of a vibrant service sector in Canada. In addition, given the growing importance of human-resource development, combined telecommunications and computer technologies can increasingly play a strategic role in education and training.

The August 1989 ruling of the Supreme Court of Canada – stating that the federal government has sole constitutional jurisdiction over all of the major telephone companies in Canada (including those previously held to be under provincial jurisdiction) – provides the opportunity for the development of an appropriate set of rules for telecommunications across the country. With the removal of Crown immunity for some companies that were previously regulated at the provincial level, there is scope for designing a single set of rules for telecommunications across the country, eliminating the inefficiencies and inequalities associated with a jurisdictionally fractured system.

A detailed prescription for a Canadian telecommunications and computer policy that would promote the development of a diversified, efficient, and high-quality service sector and of effective linkages between goods and services is far beyond the scope of this Statement. However, there is no question that Canadian telecommunications policy must evolve as the structure of the global economy changes and as new technologies appear. That evolution will necessarily involve a large number of regulatory issues and key decisions regarding standards for the content and format of the information to be exchanged. An important issue will be the extent to which competition is used to achieve the desired results.

It is also likely that regional issues will play a growing role in decision-making in this area. Natural market forces will almost certainly create the strongest pressures for the introduction of new telecommunications capabilities in the highly developed parts of the country. Those areas, which are lagging in terms of the range of telecommunications services offered, will find it increasingly difficult to compete with the more advanced regions. Policy must therefore ensure that all regions in Canada are given equal opportunity to develop information-based industries by having the necessary telecommunications capabilities in place.

12 **We therefore urge the federal and provincial governments to view the Canadian telecommunications and computer infrastructure "proactively" as a vital component of an internationally competitive, diversified, information-based economy. At least four dimensions must be considered in shaping such an infrastructure: the technological capabilities of the system; the availability of enhanced services; the cost structure; and the adoption of international standards.**

Regional Development

The labour market trends evoked in the present Statement cannot help but make the job of reducing regional disparities more difficult. Since a detailed analysis of the implications of the growth of services for regional policy was not an explicit element of our research, we offer only general observations here.

How can lagging regions improve their performance? Unfortunately, given the new economic realities, the fundamental challenge is to prevent further widening of the existing gaps –between urban and rural areas in general, and between smaller urban areas and major metropolitan centres, most of which are located in the already highly developed regions, in particular.

The development of dynamic services in the less-developed regions is constrained by the frequent lack of integration of branch plants with local service producers and by the fact that the head offices of multi-branch firms tend to be located in the highly developed regions. The possibilities for a decentralized development of dynamic services therefore appear to be limited to services that respond to the needs of locally controlled businesses, to services that have been decentralized to less costly locations by multi-branch firms, to tradable specialized services that have developed on the basis of expertise related to the local industrial base, and to services that respond to public-sector demand through procurement. With respect to the last of these, the federal Department of Supply and Services has recently initiated changes in procurement policy that appear to be based on a recognition of the role that this instrument can play in regional development. While competitive pricing should unquestionably remain as the basis for awarding contracts, efforts must be made to ensure that goods and service producers have equal opportunity to bid on government contracts, regardless of location.

Regional-development efforts should build upon the complementarities that exist between services and the regional industrial base. In this country, that base is often resource-oriented; given the particularly strong stimulative effect (suggested by our analysis) of several resource activities on the demand for services, this traditional strength of the Canadian economy may be well-suited to generating growth in dynamic services. To make this happen, firms in the resource sector – and indeed in other sectors of the regional economy – must have computer-based technologies in place. Regional lags in the diffusion of these technologies will handicap the entire regional economy because of the linkages between industries. Those concerned with regional development must, therefore, view the spread of technological change as an essential part of building the infrastructure of the 1990s and beyond.

In other cases, services based on specialized local expertise often develop in association with universities, local research centres, or other specialized facilities. Here, too, the key is to capitalize on local skills, opening the door perhaps to other markets in Canada and abroad.

It is not inconceivable that, at some point in the 21st century, new technologies – and, perhaps equally important, social innovations – will lead to more dispersed patterns of economic activity. For now, however, dynamic services remain an overwhelmingly urban phenomenon; and while subregional centres based on special skills may develop, extensive decentralization is not likely over the medium term. Therefore, regional planners must pay special attention to the health of their largest urban areas as a means of ensuring that disparities across regions do not widen. And by promoting competitiveness, especially in those services which are linked to local resource and manufacturing firms, those local firms will themselves benefit from higher-quality inputs. In that way, growth can spread throughout regions as well.

Finally, a necessary condition for regional growth will be the development of a well-educated and skilled work force. Increasingly, cities that are able to offer specialized pools of skills will attract new business activities in unique niches. Those concerned with regional development, therefore, will have to be concerned with the issues related to training and education discussed in this Statement.

Measuring the Service Economy

Economic policy would benefit from better data on service activity. Major problems have been consistently identified in the measurement of service output, productivity growth, and trade. In undertaking our research on services, we identified a number of other data problems. For example, the instruments for tracking the business cycle – such as new and unfilled orders, productive capacity, and inventories – must be reshaped to reflect more accurately an economy in which the service sector has become so important. Also, data are needed on the in-house service activities of goods-producing firms; such information would provide insights into an important component of real service employment and would make possible a better assessment of the magnitude of the contracting-out of services by goods-producing firms. To offer another example, methods of estimating productivity growth rates by sector need to be improved; estimates appear to be biased in such a way that the share of economywide productivity gains allocated to the goods sector is inflated, while the service sector's share is biased downward. As well, some of the key components of an information-based economy have yet to be defined and measured successfully; for example, there are simply no objective yardsticks for the concepts of "skill" and "knowledge."

What is required is an extension and rethinking of the measures that economists have traditionally used. We strongly support the request, made by Statistics Canada, for resources to review the national statistical base in order to improve its capacity to measure service activity. Better information on services, by improving the basis for decision-making, would, in the final analysis, benefit all Canadians.

* * * * *

The Canadian economy, along with the economies of other highly developed countries, is undergoing tremendous change. The remarkable growth of the service sector is, at the same time, both a cause and a manifestation of that change. In this Statement, we have stressed the contribution that services now make to competitiveness and overall performance – both in their own right and through their role in the production of goods. In the new interdependent economy, the distinctions between goods and services are becoming blurred, and the success of one depends on the efficiency and growth of the other.

Many Canadians still think of the service economy as "second rank" – as a source of weak productivity and bad jobs. That perception is true, but it is only half of the story. The service sector is also a source of good jobs and high productivity, providing new avenues for wealth creation and new scope for building stronger, more competitive industries.

The trends that we have described raise major challenges for both workers and employers, on the one hand, and for governments, on the other. In the face of the polarization of the labour market and of the acceleration in economic restructuring, Canadian workers must commit themselves to a life-long personal strategy of skill formation and adjustment to change. In our view, Canadian employers will play a particularly critical role in the process of adaptation to the "double-edged" labour market. They must adopt a much stronger focus on human resources by investing more in people and, where possible, by transforming bad jobs with low pay, benefits, and stability into better jobs that provide greater economic security. The slowdown in the growth of the labour force and anticipated shortages of skilled workers will create some pressure to move in that direction. The degree of change required, however, will not occur unless more employers become highly committed to the development of human resources.

While emphasizing the importance of the actions of employers and workers, the Council believes there is also an essential role for public policy in the emerging labour market. The bad-jobs side of the story is heightening the stakes for effective training and labour-adjustment programs and for other programs that influence the economic security of workers. The good-jobs side is placing new demands on Canada's education and training systems, and on industrial policies.

Ultimately, many of Canada's traditional institutions and patterns of behaviour must be reshaped by governments and market forces acting in concert to build competitive industries and to enhance the security of Canadian workers.

Comments

Peter Brophey and Chester Johnson

We are generally in agreement with this Council Statement. Our comment pertains to its treatment of the issue of adjustment policies in the case of layoff situations. While re-employment would be facilitated by the advance-notice periods called for in Recommendation 4, we do not agree with Recommendation 5, which would require all jurisdictions to establish a labour standard providing for the creation of a labour-management adjustment committee in the case of a major layoff.

We recognize the seriousness of major layoffs and the magnitude of the adjustment problems that they can pose for those workers who have lost their jobs. However, in our view, this recommendation is impractical relative to what actually happens in the marketplace. There is certainly a clear responsibility on the part of employers to do what they can to improve the re-employment chances of laid-off workers. In some instances, it may be desirable for management to work with labour to this end; in fact, this is often done on a voluntary basis by enlightened and concerned employers. Acting alone or with representatives of their work force, many employers choose to undertake redeployment, counselling, and other programs to assist displaced employees in the event of a major layoff or closure.

We do not believe, however, that an employer's response to the adjustment required in a major layoff situation should be the subject of legislation. Ultimately, then, we are concerned about the compulsory aspect of Recommendation 5 in the current Canadian environment. Domestic and overseas investors must see Canada as an attractive setting in which it is easy to do business while, at the same time, a humane safety net is maintained. In our view, this condition would be met with prevailing social benefit programs, enhanced by the advance-notice standards called for in Recommendation 4.

Graham Wilson

I agree with much of this Council Statement. However, I do not support two specific recommendations and the emphasis of the discussion surrounding a third.

I do not support Recommendation 5, which stipulates that it be legislated that, in the case of major layoffs, a committee should be required that includes management and labour representatives to develop and implement a re-employment plan. First, the recommendation is silent as to whom the representatives should be. If the Council believes that there should be a certain set of players at the table, it should be precise in identifying just what group or representatives they are suggesting. Also, while I believe that it is highly desirable for management and labour to consult in devising a fair re-employment package to make labour adjustment and relocation as painless as possible, it should not be a legislated requirement. Finally, while the text indicates that the proposal would only apply where workers must seek new employment opportunities, the proposal itself makes no such distinction. Indeed, the explanation only refers to an exception in the case where layoffs are seasonal in nature and it makes no reference to cyclical layoffs which may also be temporary.

Regarding Recommendation 6, I do not object to the recommendation as proposed but I believe that it, and the surrounding discussion on employer-based training, fail to address the most important factors that must be involved in stimulating the human-resource development efforts of Canadian firms and workers. The Statement discusses at some length what kind of instruments might be effectively used to stimulate human-resource development at the level of the firm. A number of "training triggers" are identified, including training taxes. After this review of training taxes and other types of triggers, the Statement does not recommend the institution of a universally applied standard at this time. What is lacking in the Statement, in my view, is any real discussion of what may motivate employers and employees to institute strong measures to overcome the problems of inadequate investments in training. More skills development will be undertaken by employers and employees if they recognize certain motivators that are market driven. Individual firms and workers make decisions as to what training to undertake, they carry out the activity, and they incur many of the costs. Employers will only be willing to incur these costs if they expect positive results in the form of increased productivity and profits. Workers are motivated by expected gains in income, job satisfaction, and job security. These are the triggers to training. What is required, then, are the right incentives for employers and employees to increase their education and training activities. Policy which concentrates on the real motivators should be the focus in addressing the problems of inadequate training. These motivators apply not only to big business and big labour, but also to medium- and small-size firms where a great deal more training and better training must be concentrated.

While I am in agreement with much of the logic surrounding Recommendation 7, including the principle that we must reduce the number of people who need safety nets provided by public benefit programs, I believe any proposal in this area should be precise. The recommendation includes the phrase "part-time employees with an ongoing employer attachment." Unless the meaning of that phrase were more precisely drawn so that its ramifications could be considered, I am not prepared to support this recommendation.

Project Staff

Gordon Betcherman, project leader

Marcel Bédard
Christina Caron
Surendra Gera
Norm Leckie
Kathryn McMullen
Benoît Papillon
Harry Postner
Syed Sajjadur Rahman
Tom Siedule

Juliette Beauger-Legault, secretary